Because I Was Inverted

Because I Was Inverted

Building a Strong Servant Leader Culture

Joshua Schmitz

Because I Was Inverted: Building a Strong Servant Leader Culture

Copyright © Business Expert Press, LLC, 2026

Cover design by Joshua Schmitz

Interior design by Exeter Premedia Services Private Ltd., Chennai, India

All rights reserved. No part of this publication may be reproduced, stored in a retrieval system, or transmitted in any form or by any means—electronic, mechanical, photocopy, recording, or any other—except for brief quotations, not exceeding 400 words, without the prior permission of the publisher.

First published in 2026 by
Business Expert Press, LLC
222 East 46th Street, New York, NY 10017
www.businessexpertpress.com

ISBN-13: 978-1-63742-960-0 (paperback)
ISBN-13: 978-1-63742-961-7 (e-book)

Human Resource Management and Organizational Behavior Collection

First edition: 2026

10 9 8 7 6 5 4 3 2 1

EU SAFETY REPRESENTATIVE
Mare Nostrum Group B.V.
Doelen 72
4831 GR Breda
The Netherlands
gpsr@mare-nostrum.co.uk

To my wife, my partner in life since our high school days. From the very beginning, you have been my anchor, my encourager, and my greatest source of strength. Your love and support have carried me through every season, and nothing I've accomplished would be possible without you by my side.

And to my three incredible daughters, you are my greatest gift and the legacy I am most proud to leave behind. You are smart, strong, and beautiful, each with your own unique light, and I believe with all my heart that there is nothing you cannot accomplish when you set your mind to it. Watching you grow into the women you are becoming fills me with joy, pride, and gratitude every single day.

This book is for you with the hope that the lessons shared within it reflect not only my journey in leadership but also the love, resilience, and purpose that I see in each of you. May you always know how deeply you are loved and how endlessly proud I am to be your husband and father.

Description

***Because I Was Inverted: Building a Strong Servant Leader Culture* is a fresh, story-driven guide that flips traditional leadership on its head. This book is perfect for business leaders, managers, and entrepreneurs who want to inspire trust, build strong teams, and create a workplace culture where people and performance thrive.**

Blending timeless leadership principles with memorable pop culture references from Bob Ross and *Monsters, Inc.* to Batman and even Ludacris, this book makes the mindset and tools of servant leadership both practical and engaging. Readers will discover useful strategies to foster clarity, strengthen resilience, and connect more authentically with their teams.

Through honest lessons in empathy, vulnerability, and emotional intelligence, the authors clearly demonstrate that leadership is not about power or status, but about service. This book is for anyone who wants to lead with authenticity, courage, and heart; whether you're managing a small team or guiding an entire organization.

If you're looking for a refreshing and practical take-on leadership that entertains as much as it equips, *Because I Was Inverted* is the perfect addition to your library.

Contents

Introduction: Because I Was Inverted—The Servant Leader's Mindset

Lessons in Servant Leadership and Building a Positive Business Culture

Leadership is often portrayed as a linear, upward march a career-long climb up a ladder built from authority, credentials, and control. It's a system shaped by traditional business norms: command-and-control hierarchies, polished personas, and a belief that the person at the top must always have the answers.

We're taught to equate leadership with being the expert in the room. The decision maker. The boss. Someone who drives performance by directing others, by demanding results, by wielding power. It's a model that has shaped generations of leaders and one that still dominates many organizations today.

But what if that image is not only incomplete—it's wrong?

What if real leadership isn't about climbing to the top of the ladder, but about flipping the whole structure upside down? What if the most effective leadership doesn't come from exerting control, but from embracing humility? What if the person with the greatest impact is not the one shouting orders from the front, but the one walking beside others, asking, *How can I help you succeed?*

This book was born from that question.

My Leadership Journey Started Inverted

I didn't start out as a leader in the traditional sense not by title, not by temperament, and certainly not by training. In fact, I often felt inverted like I was wired differently from the leaders I saw around me. While others projected certainty, I was full of questions. Where others seemed to lead by asserting control, I found more value in building relationships. I didn't want to bark orders; I wanted to listen, to understand, to *serve.*

Early in my career, that felt like a disadvantage. I wondered if I was missing something essential, some key leadership gene or executive instinct. But over time, something shifted. I noticed that the people I worked with didn't need someone to manage them, they needed someone to believe in them. They didn't need more pressure; they needed more purpose. And they didn't need a hero; they needed a human being.

That realization was the beginning of a new kind of leadership path for me. One built not on climbing above others, but on lifting others up.

I learned that when you invert the leadership model, when you flip the pyramid and put people first, everything changes. Team dynamics improve. Trust deepens. Innovation thrives. Culture strengthens. And yes, results follow.

What This Book Is and What It's Not

This book is a collection of the lessons I've learned along the way not from theory, but from the real-world experiences of building teams, navigating change, facing failures, and growing into leadership the hard, honest, and human way.

It's not a book about being a perfect leader. I'm not one and neither are you. But that's the point. Leadership isn't about perfection. It's about presence. It's about showing up, day after day, with integrity, vulnerability, and the willingness to put people first.

What you'll find in these pages are insights, tools, and stories that bring the principles of servant leadership to life. You'll hear about Pixar movies, 1990s rap lyrics, and breakfast clubs because leadership isn't just learned in the boardroom. It's lived in the everyday moments where we choose how to respond, how to support, and how to lead.

You'll also explore how to:

- **Cultivate a positive mindset that inspires rather than exhausts.**
- **Build trust through consistent, authentic relationships.**
- **Balance structure and flexibility to empower, not control.**

- **Communicate with empathy across personality types and situations.**
- **Lead through adversity and change without burning out yourself or your team.**

You'll laugh, reflect, and probably recognize parts of yourself: both the parts you're proud of and the parts you're still working on. That's intentional. Leadership is a lifelong process of learning and unlearning.

Why Positivity and Culture Matter Now More Than Ever

In today's workplace, the need for servant leadership has never been more urgent. Burnout is real. Disconnection is widespread. Many employees are no longer willing to tolerate toxic cultures or cold, transactional leadership. They want to feel seen, valued, and connected to something meaningful. And they deserve that.

As a leader, you have the opportunity and the responsibility to create a culture where that happens. Where people don't just survive the workweek but *thrive* in their roles. Where they're not just motivated by a paycheck, but by a shared purpose. Where they feel safe enough to speak up, strong enough to take risks, and supported enough to grow.

Creating that kind of culture isn't easy. It requires intention, self-awareness, and a willingness to lead differently. But it's worth it because when you lead with empathy and positivity, you don't just build better teams. You build better people. And in doing so, you build better results.

Let's Flip the Script

Because I was inverted, I learned that leadership is not about standing above, it's about standing alongside. It's about being a servant first, a leader second. It's about showing up with consistency, compassion, and the courage to lead from the heart.

If you've ever felt like you didn't quite fit the traditional mold, if you've ever questioned whether leadership can be something deeper, more human, better than this book is for you.

Let's challenge the old rules together. Let's redefine leadership not as a race to the top, but as a responsibility to lift others up.

Let's lead differently.
Let's lead with purpose.
Let's lead like we mean it.

Because the world doesn't need more bosses.
It needs more servant leaders.
And it needs *you*.

So, strap in, trust your wingman, and get ready to fly inverted because when you lead with heart, service, and courage, you don't just break the mold ... you break the sound barrier.

PART I

Shaping the Leader's Mindset

CHAPTER 1

A Little Bob Ross—Paint the Picture for Them

This chapter explores how servant leaders use vision like an artist uses a brush—to create clarity, possibility, and shared purpose. Drawing inspiration from Bob Ross, we'll unpack how to move from vague goals to vivid alignment.

Leadership is not a job title. It's not a business card, a LinkedIn headline, or the number of people in your reporting structure.

Leadership is a paintbrush.

And if you're going to lead people well, if you're going to inspire them, develop them, and guide them toward something greater, you need to learn how to *paint the picture for them.*

Inverted leadership, especially through the lens of servant leadership, requires vision that is shared—not just seen. This is where Bob Ross comes in.

The Art of Painting Possibility

There's a reason people still watch Bob Ross decades after he aired his last episode. It's not just nostalgia. It's not even about painting.

It's about *possibility*.

Bob Ross took blank canvases and turned them into scenes that made people *feel*. He didn't rush. He didn't criticize. He invited people in. He made them believe that they could create something beautiful even if they had never held a paintbrush in their life.

Imagine if your team felt that way about the work you do together. Imagine if, every time you rolled out a new goal, a new direction, or a new standard, they *believed* that they could help bring it to life.

They can. But only if you take the time to show them what's possible.

Why People Need a Picture

The brain is a visual processor. Studies show that people remember up to 65 percent of information when it's paired with a visual, compared to just 10–20 percent when they hear it alone.

But this isn't just about PowerPoints or diagrams.

This is about leadership communication about emotionally *anchoring* your message in something people can see, feel, and believe in.

When leaders communicate without painting a picture, they often sound like this:

"We need to be more efficient."
"Let's raise client satisfaction."
"We're going to elevate the standard."

But to your team, that's just noise. Abstract. Unclear. Disconnected.

Try this instead:Right now, our clients wait an average of 12 minutes before being greeted. Imagine we create a flow where, no matter how busy we are, someone is at the front within the first 2 minutes. They walk in, and immediately they feel cared for. That's what we're aiming for. That's what we build together.

Now they see it. Now they get it. Now they *want* it.

Research shows that people recall about twice as much information when it's paired with meaningful visuals compared to text alone (Nelson, Reed, and Walling, 1976; Paivio, 1991). In leadership terms: if your goal lives only in words, half of it will be forgotten before your team even leaves the meeting.

Tools to Paint the Picture as a Leader

Whether you're guiding a frontline team or shaping organizational culture, these leadership tools help you paint more vivid, effective pictures:

1. **Tell Stories**
   Real stories anchor abstract goals in real-world emotion. Share wins. Share setbacks. Share your own experiences with vulnerability.

"I remember when I first started as a tech I felt invisible. That's why I want to build a culture where no role feels forgotten."

2. **Use Whiteboards (Real or Virtual)**
   Physically drawing out workflows, goals, or changes engages people visually and cognitively. Don't underestimate a whiteboard and some markers. Simplicity wins.
3. **Walk the Process**
   Take your team through what the future looks like. What does it feel like to work here after this change? What will clients notice? What will *you* notice?
   "Picture this: You walk in at 8 a.m. and everything is prepped. Everyone knows their role. No one's rushing. You're confident. That's the goal."
4. **Invite Contribution**
   Ask your team to paint with you. Let them offer color, detail, and dimension.

"What does excellence look like to you?"
"What's a small change that would make your day smoother?"
"What do you think is missing from our current canvas?"

When people contribute, they commit.

Clarity Is the Compass

Clarity isn't a luxury in leadership, it's a necessity.

When you paint a clear picture:

- People make better decisions without constant guidance.
- Teams become aligned, because they're pointed in the same direction.
- Motivation increases, because the "why" is no longer hidden.

And this isn't just theory, a meta-analysis of over 23,000 employees found that *role clarity* was significantly correlated with higher job satisfaction, better performance, and lower turnover intentions (Tubre and

Collins, 2000). In other words, the clearer the picture, the better the results and the longer people stay to keep painting it.

Unclear leaders create uncertain teams.
Uncertain teams create inconsistent results.

This doesn't mean you have to have all the answers. But you do need to define the *destination*. You need to light the path. You need to say:

"This is where we're going. This is why it matters. And this is how we'll get there together."

A Story from the Floor: The Power of the Picture

At one point, I was helping a clinic that had been struggling with burnout. High turnover. Low morale. Constant tension between departments.

They asked me, "How do we fix the culture?"

I didn't give them a policy manual. I gave them a picture.

We brought the whole team into a meeting and did a creative exercise. I asked:

"If our clinic were a place where you *loved* to work, what would it look like when you walked in?"

And they told me:

- "Smiling faces."
- "A clean breakroom."
- "People actually saying good morning."
- "No blaming just helping."
- "Patients getting care without chaos."

We wrote those down. We *drew* them on a big poster board. That became our vision canvas. Every change we made after that tied back to that picture. It wasn't just an ideal, it was their picture. It meant something.

Three months later, turnover slowed. Engagement rose. The mood shifted. And it all started because they could finally *see* what they were working toward.

Let Them Hold the Brush

Bob Ross didn't just paint. He taught people how to paint.

As servant leaders, our job isn't to be the only visionary; it's to empower others to become visionaries themselves. To cultivate clarity, yes, but also creativity and collaboration.

Your people want to contribute. They want their fingerprints on the final product. So let them:

- Share decisions.
- Solve problems.
- Shape culture.

And when they do, affirm them:

"That color you added changed the whole tone. I'm glad you spoke up."

When the Picture Changes

Leadership also means being willing to admit when the picture shifts.

Sometimes the first version of the vision isn't right. Or it no longer fits the evolving landscape. That's okay. In fact, it's necessary.

What matters is transparency. When you need to revise the picture:

- Be honest.
- Acknowledge the change.
- Involve the team in redrawing it.

Bob Ross famously said, "We don't make mistakes. We just have happy little accidents." Some of your best leadership moments will come from changes you didn't expect if you invite your team into the process of repainting.

From Brushstrokes to Blueprint—Leading With Vision, Not Vague

If leadership is a canvas, then vague goals are fog.

No one paints clearly in the fog.

You can hand your team the highest-quality brushes, premium paints, and a beautiful studio, but if they can't see where they're going, frustration builds fast.

Servant leadership isn't just about inspiring people emotionally, it's about making the mission visible, step by step. It's about transforming ideas into imagery, then imagery into action.

Let's talk about how to move from impressionist leadership (vague but well-intended) to intentional leadership (clear, compelling, and collaborative).

The Fog of Ambiguity

Have you ever told your team to:

- "Take more initiative."
- "Raise the standard."
- "Be more accountable."
- "Own the client experience."

Those aren't wrong statements, they're just half-painted.

When goals are abstract, people freeze. Or worse, they guess. And when they guess, they often aim in the wrong direction, leaving everyone frustrated.

Clarity is kindness. Ambiguity is anxiety.

Your job as a leader is to *defog* the frame.

Paint Like a Communicator, Not Just a Creator

Bob Ross didn't just create art; he talked you through it.

"This is a happy little tree … maybe it lives next to this stream. And maybe there's a friend here for it."

He *narrated possibility* while he painted. He helped you *feel like you were part of it.*

As a leader, your team doesn't just need vision, they need narration.

Don't just *draw the picture.*

Describe what it looks like, sounds like, and feels like.

If you want your team to embrace a new direction, you need to:

- Walk them through it.
- Connect it to what they care about.
- Make it feel human, real, and achievable.

The "Three-Frame" Vision Method

One way to make your vision real is to use the "Three-Frame Model," a mental tool you can use in meetings, 1:1s, or presentations to paint a clear before–during–after picture.

Frame 1: "Where We Are"

Start with reality. Describe the current scene.

"Right now, we have great people working really hard, but our systems are clunky. Clients are feeling that friction, and so are we."

Be honest but not condemning.

Frame 2: "Where We're Going"

Paint the desired future in detail.

"Imagine this: every client gets a personal welcome call the day before their appointment. When they arrive, their records are ready. Our team isn't rushing; they're connecting."

Let them see it. Let them want it.

Frame 3: "How We Get There"

Then build the bridge.

"To get there, we'll be simplifying our intake process, cross-training on phone duties, and introducing a new morning huddle to sync as a team."

This model helps your team contextualize the journey and see their role within it.

Vision Without Execution Is Wallpaper

Bob Ross didn't just show you a finished picture, he showed you how to build it layer by layer.

Likewise, leadership vision can't just live in a speech or strategy deck. It needs to show up:

- In how meetings are structured.
- In what behaviors are rewarded.
- In the systems that support the work.

If the way you operate contradicts the vision you speak, trust will erode.

So, when you paint a picture:

- Check that your priorities align with it.
- Review if your processes support it.
- Adjust your own actions to reflect it.

Vision isn't a mural. It's a mirror.

"Every Tree Needs a Shadow"—Addressing the Hard Stuff, Too

Ross often said, *You need dark to show light.*
That principle applies to leadership.

If everything is painted in positivity with no acknowledgment of hardship, people will tune you out. Why? Because it doesn't reflect their reality.

Don't be afraid to:

- Talk about past failures or frustrations.
- Name real obstacles.
- Express empathy for what the team has experienced.

Then and only then can you meaningfully introduce the better future you're inviting them to.

Contrast creates clarity. Shadow gives dimension.

Making Vision a Two-Way Brush

Servant leadership invites others to *copaint* the picture. Not just to understand it, but to shape it.

Here are three ways to make your team part of the process:

1. **Run a "Sketch Session"**
   Ask your team:
   - *If we were doing our best work six months from now, what would that look like?*
   - *What would a five-star experience feel like from your role?*

   Write their words down. Show them they matter.
2. **Create a Living Vision Board**
   Digitally or on the wall, collect:
   - Images
   - Words
   - Phrases
   - Team-generated ideas

   Update it monthly. Let it evolve. Let them own it.
3. **Nominate "Vision Carriers"**
   Identify two to three people from different roles who embody the culture you're building.

   Ask them to be part of weekly huddles or check-ins—to reflect, suggest, and amplify the picture in peer conversations.

   People follow people more than they follow plans.

Leadership Is a Visual Sport

At the end of the day, leadership is visual.

Not because everyone needs a drawing—but because everyone needs something they can *see themselves in.*

It's your job to:

- Translate vision into visuals.
- Show them the path.
- Include their brushstrokes.
- And celebrate the moments they color outside the lines with something better than what you imagined.

Final Thoughts: Every Leader Is an Artist

You don't need to be an actual painter. But you *are* an artist.

Every conversation is a brushstroke.
Every decision is a line of shadow or light.
Every act of service shapes the bigger picture.

So slow down. Explain. Inspire. Invite.
Paint the picture.

Let people see where they're going. Let them believe in what they're building. Let them hold the brush. And don't forget to leave space for a few happy little trees.

Reflective Exercise: Pick Up the Brush

Take 15–20 minutes in a quiet space with no distractions. This is your moment to reflect, visualize, and clarify your leadership canvas.

1. **What's Your Current Canvas?**

   Think about your team, business, or organization right now.

   - How would you honestly describe the current "picture" your team sees?
   - Is it clear? Confusing? Inspiring? Stressful?
   - What colors are most dominant in your culture today? (E.g., urgency, burnout, collaboration, learning, etc.)

   Write a few sentences that describe the scene as it currently exists.

2. **What Picture Do You Want to Paint?**

   Now imagine 6–12 months from now. Things are working well. People are engaged. The mission feels alive.

   - What does it look like when your team is thriving?
   - What are people doing?
   - What's the energy in the room?
   - What do clients or customers notice when they interact with your business?

   Sketch it in words. Paint it with emotion and detail.

3. **What's Missing From the Frame?**

   Every picture needs structure, light, and balance.

   - What's missing right now from your team's understanding of your vision?
   - Where might you be assuming that clarity exists when it doesn't?
   - Are there any "happy little accidents" that need to be reframed as opportunities?

   List two to three things that you want to clarify better for your team starting this week.

4. **Who Needs a Brush?**

   Servant leadership invites others to help shape the vision.

   - Who on your team has insight, perspective, or creative input into which you haven't yet tapped?
   - How could you involve them in building the next version of your team's culture, goals, or processes?

   List one to two people whom you can invite into the next planning conversation, meeting, or decision.

5. **Your Next Brushstroke**

   What's one thing you will do this week to *paint the picture* for your team more clearly:

   - A story you'll tell?
   - A visual you'll draw?
   - A conversation you'll have?
   - A question you'll ask?

   Write your next step here:

"You can do anything you want to do. This is your world."

—Bob Ross

Just like Bob, your leadership doesn't need to be flashy, it needs to be *intentional.* Clarity, care, and creativity are your brushes. Now pick them up and start painting.

CHAPTER 2

It Worked for Monsters, Inc.—Laughter Versus Fear

This chapter explores the surprising leadership wisdom hidden in Monsters, Inc.*; that joy, not fear, is the most powerful and sustainable energy source for teams. While fear-based leadership can drive short-term results, it ultimately drains morale, stifles creativity, and increases burnout. Through research, real-world stories, and actionable tools, you'll learn how to recognize fear-based patterns, build a culture of psychological safety, and lead with intentional joy. The L.E.A.P. framework (Lead with Levity, Express Emotion, Appreciate Often, Play with Purpose) gives you practical steps to energize your team, deepen trust, and turn laughter into a leadership advantage.*

There's a moment in *Monsters, Inc.* that's pure genius simple enough for kids to grasp, but profound enough for leaders to build cultures around.

For years, the monsters powered their world by collecting the screams of frightened children. It worked, but it was heavy, draining, and built on fear. Then they discovered something surprising:

Laughter was not only more powerful; it was more sustainable.

It produced more energy. It generated joy. And most importantly, it transformed the monsters themselves.

It's funny how close this hits to home in the business world. Because many leaders, even well-meaning ones, still operate in "scream mode." They rely on pressure, urgency, control, and fear to push results. It works, yes but at what cost?

As servant leaders, we have the opportunity to do something far more powerful.

We can choose laughter.

We can choose joy.

We can build a culture that energizes, not exhausts.

Fear Works, But It's Toxic

Let's be honest. Fear gets short-term results. Just like the screams in *Monsters, Inc.*, fear-based leadership can drive compliance, urgency, and effort at first.

- "If we don't hit this number, people are losing jobs."
- "Don't mess this up or you'll be on probation."
- "I expect you to be here early if you want to stay on this team."

Sound familiar?

Fear creates a high-alert culture. People move quickly. They avoid mistakes. But they also:

- Stop taking risks.
- Avoid ownership.
- Shut down creativity.
- Burn out—fast.

Over time, fear-based leadership builds a team that looks productive on the surface, but is emotionally checked out underneath. They're showing up, but they're drained.

Just like the scream collectors at *Monsters, Inc.*, they're working harder and harder to get smaller and smaller returns. *Fear-based cultures are expensive, disengaged employees cost companies an estimated $450–$550 billion annually in lost productivity in the US alone.*

(Source: Gallup, 2022)

Why Joy Wins (Even in Business)

When Mike and Sulley discovered laughter, everything changed. Their energy skyrocketed. Their world brightened. And the monsters themselves became better, more connected, more human.

That's the magic of joy.

In business, joy doesn't mean goofing off or avoiding accountability. It means creating a workplace where people:

- Feel safe to speak up.
- Know they're valued beyond their output.
- Have moments of fun, laughter, and levity.
- Work toward something meaningful.

When laughter becomes part of your workplace culture:

- Teams collaborate more easily.
- Trust deepens.
- Resilience increases.
- Turnover drops.
- Innovation grows.

Teams that intentionally use humor and laughter experience 10 percent greater creativity and solve problems 20 percent faster than those that don't.
(Source: Association for Applied and Therapeutic Humor, 2021)

Joy isn't just a "perk." It's a productivity engine.

The Science Behind It

This isn't just Pixar storytelling. There's actual science to back it up.

- Laughter triggers the release of endorphins, improving mood and making people more open to connection.
- Psychological safety, a concept pioneered by Harvard researcher Amy Edmondson, shows that teams perform better when they feel safe to take interpersonal risks.
- Positive emotion broadens thinking. Barbara Fredrickson's Broaden-and-Build theory explains how joy helps people see more possibilities, solve problems creatively, and build long-term capacity.

In short? Positivity isn't fluff, it's a competitive advantage.

How Fear Shows Up (Even When We Don't Realize It)

Not all fear-based leadership is loud or aggressive. Sometimes it's subtle:

- The *cold silence* after a mistake.
- Withholding praise unless perfection is reached.
- Micromanaging under the guise of "standards."
- Using pressure as the only motivator.

As servant leaders, we have to *invert* that approach.

Instead of "How do I get more out of my people?"
Ask: "How do I pour more into them so they thrive?"

That's the shift. That's the power. That's laughter over fear.

Culture Check: Is Your Team Laughing?

You can tell a lot about the workplace by the sound it makes.

- Are there moments of laughter?
- Do people joke (respectfully) with each other?
- Can your team breathe during the day?
- Is fun allowed or only tolerated on Fridays?

Laughter is a culture indicator. You don't need ping-pong tables or office parties to make joy part of your workplace. It's about emotional freedom. It's about bringing humanity back into the daily grind.

Leadership Tools to Shift From Fear to Joy

1. **Lead With Warmth**
   Before you worry about being respected, focus on being relatable. Trust flows faster from warmth than authority.
   Action: Start every team huddle with one light, human moment. A personal check-in, a funny client story, a moment of gratitude.

2. **Celebrate Out Loud**

   If fear punishes mistakes loudly, then joy should celebrate wins loudly.

   Action: Create a "caught doing good" board or Slack thread where anyone can shout out a teammate. Model it. Keep it consistent.

3. **Inject Humor With Intention**

   Laughter doesn't have to come from jokes; it can come from moments of shared humanity.

   Action: Let yourself be seen. Tell stories of your own failures. Laugh at yourself when appropriate. It gives others permission to let down their guard.

4. **Recognize Emotional Labor**

   Especially in caregiving industries like veterinary medicine, the work is *emotionally heavy*. Joy becomes a pressure valve.

   Action: Build in moments for decompression like daily "debrief and breathe" moments or a weekly light-hearted trivia break.

5. **Replace Fear With Curiosity**

   Instead of responding to underperformance with punishment, get curious.

   Action: Ask, "What's getting in your way?" or "What support would help you feel more confident in this area?"

   Curiosity dissolves fear and invites growth.

A Real-Life Example: The Clinic That Learned to Laugh Again

I once worked with a clinic where the culture was rigid. The team was good—but they were exhausted. Morale was low. Smiles were rare. Turnover was growing.

The leader well-intentioned but intense realized that while expectations were clear, the environment was cold.

We started small.

- A "fun fact" of the week during meetings.
- A "high-five" wall by the breakroom.
- Permission to take five-minute dance breaks on tough days (yep, even if clients could hear the music).

Within a month, people were *laughing again.* Clients started commenting on the positive energy. The team was still working hard—but the *weight* had shifted.

Laughter didn't replace the work. It *fueled* it.

Leadership Reflections: Ask Yourself

- Am I leading from inspiration or obligation?
- Do my team members smile during the workday? Do I?
- Where might fear be hiding in our systems, habits, or language?
- What small moment of laughter or joy could I introduce this week?

The Monster Behind the Mirror—How We Accidentally Lead With Fear (and How to Flip It)

There's a moment in *Monsters, Inc.* that gets easily overlooked. It's subtle, but powerful: Sulley, once the top scarer, realizes the very thing that once made him great, his roar terrifies someone he cares about.

It's a quiet scene. Boo is scared of him.

That's the moment the game changes not because of new data or a quarterly report, but because Sulley sees the cost of fear up close. He realizes that *what works* isn't the same as *what's right.*

Many leaders today are still roaring without realizing who they're scaring. Not intentionally. But reflexively. Because that's how they were led. Because it gets results. Because no one ever told them joy was an option.

So, let's flip the script. Let's talk about how to recognize when fear is running your playbook and how to replace it with sustainable, contagious joy.

The Fear Formula: What It Looks Like in Real Life

Fear-based leadership doesn't always come with yelling or slamming doors. Often, it's much more subtle and more socially acceptable.

Here's what the *Fear Formula* looks like in the workplace:

1. **Expectations without empathy**
   - "Get it done. I don't care how."
2. **Deadlines without dialogue**
   - "This needs to be done by Friday. End of story."
3. **Correction without connection**
   - "This wasn't good enough. Fix it."
4. **Standards without shared purpose**
   - "This is what corporate wants. Just do it."

This approach may seem productive. But it's emotionally bankrupt. It builds teams that:

- Work for approval, not from passion.
- Avoid feedback because it feels like a threat.
- Say yes, but mean "I'm just surviving this."

As Sulley learned, even success feels hollow when it's built on other people's anxiety.

The Joy Framework—Building Energy, Not Exhaustion

So, what's the antidote? Let's introduce a framework we use in servant leadership circles called **L.E.A.P.** —four simple lenses to build a laughter-powered culture that energizes instead of exhausts.

L—Lead With Levity

Levity isn't about being silly. It's about *making space for lightness.* People work better when they're not holding their breath.

Try this: Begin your next meeting with a "nonwork win."
"What made you laugh this weekend?" "What's something small that brought you joy?"

It resets the nervous system. It signals humanity. It creates connection.

E—Express Emotion Freely

We often say, "Leave your emotions at the door." But that's like asking people to take off their heads and hearts before they clock in.

A joy-first culture doesn't suppress emotion. It *channels* it.

Try this: Normalize naming emotion in check-ins.

"What's your energy like today, 1–10?" "What's one word for how you're feeling?"

The more you understand how people feel, the more you can lead them effectively.

A—Appreciate Loud, Often, and Real

Recognition doesn't have to be fancy. But it does have to be *felt*.

Don't just say "good job." Say, "The way you handled that upset client with calm and kindness—that's exactly what great care looks like."

Try this: Create a "Gratitude Loop" where each person starts or ends their week by thanking one teammate for something specific.

Appreciation feeds joy. Consistently.

P—Play With Purpose

"Play" doesn't mean wasting time. It means *giving space for creativity, experimentation, and personality*.

Let people bring their quirks, their style, their full selves.

Try this: Let each team member design one small change to their workspace or process that brings them joy and then implement it.

When people feel freedom to contribute playfully, they engage with deeper purpose.

Joy Isn't a Perk—It's an Efficiency Multiplier

Let's be clear: joy is not a distraction from productivity. It *accelerates* it.

In fact, teams with high positive emotion experience:

- **Twenty-three percent higher profitability.**
- **Thirty-one percent higher productivity.**
- **Thirty-seven percent less absenteeism.**

(Source: Gallup + *Harvard Business Review* studies on workplace positivity.)

Why?

Because joy *frees the mind.*

It opens up creative thinking, faster collaboration, and deeper loyalty. People want to work in places where they *feel like themselves*. And when they do, they're not just compliant. They're committed.

Culture in Action: A Joyful Pivot at a Critical Moment

Let me tell you about a surgical team at a specialty practice I worked with.

They were struggling with stress, conflict, and miscommunication. One tech said during a feedback session, "I just feel like a cog in the machine. No one even knows who I am anymore."

Ouch.

The leadership team took it to heart. They didn't roll out a new mission statement. They rolled out joy.

Here's what they did:

- **Personal playlist Fridays**: One team member chose a playlist each Friday (clean and fun) to bring their personality into the operating room.
- **One-minute gratitude rounds** during preop: Each person had to thank one other for something in the past week; big or small.
- **Postprocedure debrief snacks** with a question-of-the-day: "What's one thing that made you smile this week?"

Three months in?

- Retention was up.
- Efficiency improved.
- And the tone? Totally different.

They didn't remove the pressure they just added joy.

Leadership Self-Reflection: Are You the Scarer or the Laugher?

Let's be honest. We all have moments where we default to control, pressure, or criticism. It's human. But we don't have to live there.

Ask yourself:

- Do my team members laugh more or sigh more?
- Do I invite openness or avoid it?
- Am I more likely to correct or connect?
- Would I want to work for me?

Tough questions, but necessary ones.

Because self-awareness is what keeps us from becoming the very monster we never meant to be.

Final Thoughts: Joy Is an Energy Source

Monsters, Inc. taught us that there's more power in laughter than in fear. Pixar made it cute, but the principle is real.

You get to decide what fuels your business:

- Fear or freedom.
- Pressure or possibility.
- Compliance or connection.

Joy scales.

Laughter echoes.

And teams that feel safe to be themselves will give you their best work not because they have to, but because they *want* to.

Choose joy.

Model joy.

And when in doubt laugh a little. It's good for the mission.

Reflective Exercise: Building a Joy-First Culture

Take time to work through these questions to apply this chapter to your own team and leadership.

1. **How is fear currently showing up in your leadership or culture?**
   Write two to three ways by which fear might be unintentionally influencing behavior or communication.
2. **What moments of joy or laughter do you remember recently at work?**
   Describe one moment of levity or joy that stuck with you. What made it meaningful?
3. **What systems, rituals, or traditions could you build to promote joy?**
   List two things you could try this month to make laughter part of the workplace rhythm.
4. **How can you model lightness without losing professionalism?**
   Write one to two ways by which you can bring humor, vulnerability, or warmth into your next team interaction.
5. **Your next joyful brushstroke:**
   What's one thing you'll do this week to replace fear with laughter or stress with lightness?

"It's laughter we're after."—*Monsters, Inc.*

So, go ahead, be the kind of leader who knows when to laugh, how to lift, and why joy belongs in every room you lead.

CHAPTER 3

My Precious—The Gollum Effect

When leaders cling too tightly to control, expertise, or identity, they stifle their teams and risk stagnation. This chapter explores the "Gollum Effect" a leadership trap where good intentions morph into possessiveness and offers a path forward through empowerment, delegation, and trust. You'll discover how letting go isn't losing value, but multiplying it, and why servant leaders must share their power to build lasting impact.

There's a moment in *The Lord of the Rings* that has transcended fantasy and pop culture where Gollum, once Sméagol, curls around the Ring of Power and mutters obsessively:

"My precious ..."

His voice trembles with possession. His identity has become inseparable from the thing he's clinging to. The ring isn't just powerful, it's corrosive. It isolates him, consumes him, and blinds him to reality. The more he protects it, the more it destroys him.

Welcome to the Gollum Effect in leadership.

It's what happens when leaders grip so tightly to control, status, knowledge, or even certain tasks that they begin to lose themselves and undermine the very culture they're trying to build.

This chapter is about identifying and overcoming the tendency to hoard what should be shared: power, information, ownership, and trust. It's about servant leadership's call to *release* rather than *clutch*, *share* rather than *guard*, and *develop* rather than *dominate*.

Because *my precious* thinking? It has no place in a culture of empowerment.

What Is the Gollum Effect?

In psychology, we might call this overidentification with a role, resource, or responsibility but let's keep it simple.

The Gollum Effect happens when:

- Leaders hoard knowledge, not wanting others to "do it as well as I do."
- Managers refuse to delegate because they're afraid of losing control or relevance.
- Founders overprotect their ideas or systems, stunting their team's growth.
- Individuals tie their identity too closely to one skill, tool, or piece of the business.

It may start with good intentions protecting quality, efficiency, or company values, but left unchecked, it leads to:

- Bottlenecks in decision making
- Micromanagement
- Team disengagement
- Stalled development and innovation

Just like the ring, the things we think give us control eventually control *us*.

How the Gollum Effect Shows Up at Work

Here are common phrases that often signal a "My Precious" mindset:

- "It's just easier if I do it myself."
- "No one else really knows how to do this right."
- "I don't want to lose visibility by giving that away."
- "I'll train them later, when things slow down."
- "They're not ready yet."

Let's translate those into what your team might hear instead:

- "I don't trust you."
- "You'll never be as good as me."
- "Your growth isn't worth my time."
- "This isn't your lane stay out."

And yet, these phrases often *don't* come from arrogance. They come from fear:

- Fear of becoming replaceable
- Fear of irrelevance
- Fear of losing quality
- Fear of letting go

But here's the truth: holding on too tightly is the fastest path to stagnation.

The Culture You Create When You Cling

The Gollum Effect isn't just about what you lose as a leader, it's about what your *culture* loses.

Every time a leader grips too tightly to their "precious," they unintentionally send out silent but powerful signals that ripple through the team. These unspoken messages shape expectations, behaviors, and emotional safety.

Here's the hidden cost: When leaders hoard, teams shrink.

They stop speaking up.
They stop experimenting.
They stop caring beyond what they're told to do.

Research shows that leaders who micromanage and fail to delegate reduce team productivity by up to 30 percent, largely due to decision bottlenecks and lost initiative.

(Source: *Harvard Business Review*, 2016)

Why? Because they've learned that ownership isn't available here. That growth is gated. That trust must be earned again and again, but it's rarely reciprocated.

And even worse: They might start modeling the same behavior.

The Gollum Effect is contagious.

The "Mini-Gollums" You Didn't Mean to Create

Culture cascades from the top. If your team watches you clutch at control, they'll often do the same, especially those aspiring to leadership themselves.

Here's how that plays out:

- A team lead stops training junior staff out of fear they'll outperform her.
- A senior tech gets territorial over workflows and resents newcomers asking questions.
- A new manager copies your "I'll just handle it" habits instead of learning to delegate.

Suddenly, your whole team is swimming in scarcity, not collaboration.

What began as *your* fear becomes *their* norm.

What Teams Really Want: Ownership, Not Overhead

Most team members don't want to *take* your job. They want to *do* their job with pride.

They want to:

- Contribute meaningfully.
- Understand the "why" behind what they're doing.
- Make decisions that matter.
- Be trusted to try, even if it's imperfect.

They want to grow not necessarily up the ladder, but *into* their role, into their strengths, and into confidence.

When you give them room to do that, something powerful happens: They start to act like owners.

And when people act like owners, they protect the culture, solve problems faster, and build stronger relationships with clients and each other.

They stop waiting to be told.
They start stepping up.

Companies with high employee empowerment scores outperform competitors by 21 percent in profitability.

(Source: Gallup, 2017)

What Letting Go Really Looks Like (It's Not Abandonment)

Letting go doesn't mean checking out.

Some leaders swing too far in the opposite direction: burned out from years of over functioning, they dump responsibilities without direction, support, or care.

That's not empowerment. That's abandonment.

Servant leadership is about *intentional transfer* of skills, trust, and authority.

It's not "Here, you deal with it."
It's "Here's why these matters. Let me walk alongside you until you're ready to lead it yourself."

Think of it like gardening:

- You don't yank the plant out and toss it in a new pot.
- You *prepare* the soil, *plant* the seed, *water* it consistently, and *trust* it will grow.

True delegation is not just about getting tasks off your plate; it's about growing capacity in others.

Letting Go as Emotional Labor

Here's the truth no one tells you:
Letting go can feel like grief.

Especially if you've built something from scratch or spent years becoming "the go-to" for something.

There's a real emotional cost to releasing what once defined your value.

But servant leaders process that grief *without projecting it* onto others. They don't make team members feel guilty for doing what they were invited to do. They don't hover, sabotage, or silently resent the success of others.

Instead, they acknowledge the shift.
They mourn it privately if needed.
And then they celebrate the growth they helped make possible.

Because that's what mature leadership looks like.

Why We Hold On: The Psychology of Possession in Leadership

To truly understand the Gollum Effect, we must go beneath the surface.

Clinging isn't always about ego; it's often about fear, identity, and unmet needs.

Most leaders don't wake up one morning and decide to hoard power or micromanage.
They *drift* into it.

Over time, our roles, responsibilities, and reputations intertwine so tightly that we forget where the job ends and where *we* begin.

In psychology, this is called **role fusion** when your sense of worth becomes fused with what you do or control.
The result? Any challenge to the way you work feels personal, not procedural.

When someone else steps in, you don't just see a change in the process, you feel a threat to self.

That's why even high-performing, emotionally intelligent leaders can slip into possessiveness. It's not a lack of skill. It's an unexamined attachment.

Here are three of the most common roots of leadership overattachment:

1. **Fear of Obsolescence**
   Many leaders have spent years mastering a skill or system. The idea that someone else could now perform it just as well or better feels like you're being erased. But true legacy isn't being the *only one* who can; it's being the *one who taught others how.*
2. **Comfort in Competence**
   When things feel uncertain, we all run back to what we're good at. That comfort can become a cage. A manager who's excellent at solving problems may unconsciously keep solving instead of teaching, because solving feels safe — and teaching feels vulnerable.
3. **Perfection as Protection**
   Some leaders cling because excellence is their armor. "If I do it myself, it won't fail." But that perfectionism drains both creativity and trust. Growth doesn't happen through flawless control; it happens through courageous release.

Recognizing these roots isn't about guilt, it's about grace.

You can't release what you don't first acknowledge. When you name your fear, it loses its hold.

As leadership author John Maxwell says, *You must give up to go up.*

Servant leaders understand that giving up control is not weakness,
it's wisdom.
It's the moment you trade certainty for scale.

What you hand off thoughtfully can grow beyond what you could have managed alone.

The Servant Leader's Inversion

Inverted leadership flips the traditional model of power. Instead of guarding the throne, servant leaders give away their power to build others up.

They ask:

- "Who else could own this?"
- "How can I share the spotlight?"
- "What am I holding too tightly that could become someone else's growth opportunity?"

They understand this paradox:

The more you give away, the more influence you actually gain.

Because when you develop others, empower others, and invite others into responsibility, *your value multiplies* not because you control everything, but because you cultivate something bigger than yourself.

Real-World Examples of the Gollum Effect

The "Only I Know How" Technician

A lead technician in a thriving clinic refuses to teach anyone else how to calibrate the anesthesia machine. It's not malicious, it's pride and perfectionism. But when she's on vacation and a pet needs emergency surgery, no one can do it. The whole team freezes.

Outcome? Risk to the patient. Stress for the team. Burnout for the tech who "has" to be there all the time.

The "Can't Let Go" Practice Manager

A practice manager continues to run payroll, control scheduling, and make every hiring decision, even after hiring a capable assistant manager. Her justification? "If I let that go, what's left for me to do?"

Outcome? Her assistant stagnates. The manager burns out. The team sees a culture of control, not trust.

The Impact of Letting Go

Now let's flip the script.

The Empowered New Grad

A medical director at a large clinic invites a new grad DVM to colead a wellness initiative. She gives them space to explore, make decisions, even fail. The result? That doctor becomes a linchpin in the practice and stays for five years.

The Shared Spotlight

A regional director starts every meeting by having someone else lead a five-minute "spotlight moment" to share a win, insight, or initiative. Over time, these meetings become collaborative, not top-down. The team starts owning solutions before she even needs to intervene.

> Letting go doesn't mean losing value.
> It means creating space for others to rise.

The Paradox of Power: How Letting Go Strengthens Influence

There's a strange paradox at the heart of great leadership: the moment you stop grasping for control is the moment you begin to lead with it. True power isn't about accumulation, it's about circulation. When leaders hoard authority, trust, or visibility, those things stagnate. But when they're shared, they multiply.

Think about the leaders who made the biggest difference in your life. They didn't make you feel smaller; they made you feel seen. They didn't guard every decision; they invited you into them. They didn't lead to be *needed*; they led to make *others capable.*

That's the essence of inverted, servant-minded leadership. It transforms hierarchy into humanity. It shifts the question from "How do I protect what I've built?" to "How do I build something that no longer needs protecting?"; because real leadership isn't about being indispensable. It's about being instrumental.

When you release the need to prove your worth, you free others to find theirs. When you share authority, you strengthen alignment. When you trust others with real responsibility, you give them dignity and that's what turns followers into leaders.

The paradox of power is that influence grows in direct proportion to humility. It's not found in clutching tighter, but in opening wider. And the mark of a truly great leader is not how much they hold, but how much they've given away and what still thrives after they've stepped aside.

Tools to Overcome the Gollum Effect

If you're starting to see some Gollum tendencies in yourself or your team (don't worry, we all have them), here are some tools to help you release the ring and lead with purpose.

1. **Conduct a "Let Go" Audit**
   Ask yourself:
   - What am I doing that someone else could be trained to do?
   - Where am I the bottleneck?
   - What do I fear would happen if I gave this away?

   Make a list of two to three responsibilities that you could begin delegating or teaching today.
2. **Teach, Don't Just Tell**
   Delegation isn't dumping it's developing.

   "Watch me → Do it with me → Do it solo → Teach someone else"

   Use the four-step model to transfer knowledge with confidence and accountability.
3. **Reframe Replacement as Legacy**
   What if letting go isn't about being replaced but being multiplied?
   Ask:
   - "How does building this person up create impact beyond me?"
   - "What will this look like in six months when they've mastered it?"

4. **Celebrate Shared Wins**
   Publicly recognize when someone takes ownership of something you once held. Celebrate their success.
   "It's awesome to see Sarah leading scheduling now. A few months ago, I was doing that and she's made it better."
5. **Normalize Mistakes During Transfer**
   You will cringe the first time someone does something *differently* than you. That's normal.
   But remember done is better than perfect. And growth requires grace.

Reflection: What's Your Ring?

- Is it your calendar?
- Your inbox?
- Your relationships with VIP clients?
- Your way of writing protocols?
- Your presence in every meeting?

Ask yourself: *What am I gripping that needs to be given away?*
Because until you release it, it's holding you back too.

Final Thoughts: Identity Beyond Ownership

Gollum forgot who he was before he found the ring.

Servant leaders remember who they are without the things they manage.
You are not your title. You are not your process. You are not your control.

You are a cultivator, a multiplier, a guide.
Your real legacy is what you *give away* not what you hoard.

So the next time you catch yourself clutching tightly to your "precious," pause. Take a breath. And ask:

"Is this mine to hold … or mine to release?"

Because when you release it, you rise.
And so does everyone around you.

And sometimes, the smallest act of letting go of releasing your "precious" is what frees you to become the leader you were meant to be.

Reflective Exercise: Releasing the Ring

Take 15–20 minutes to complete this self-assessment and unlock areas for growth.

1. **Inventory Your "Precious"**
   What are three things in your role that you're holding onto tightly?
   Be honest. These are likely tasks, responsibilities, or relationships you don't want to delegate.
2. **Identify the Fear**
   For each item, ask: *What am I afraid will happen if I let this go? Write your answers below each.*
3. **Shift the Lens**
   What might actually happen if you *do* let go?
   Describe the positive outcomes that could arise for your team, business, or personal well-being.
4. **Take Action**
   Pick *one* "ring" to release this month. Create a simple transition plan:
   - Who will take it on?
   - What training or support do they need?
   - How will you follow up without taking it back?

   Write your plan below.
5. **Write Your Release Statement**
   Close this exercise by writing a short, personal leadership statement:
   "I am not defined by what I hold. I lead by what I build in others. Today, I choose to release ________, so I can empower ________."

"Even the smallest person can change the course of the future."—
Galadriel, The Lord of the Rings

And sometimes, the smallest act of letting go can create the largest ripple of growth.

CHAPTER 4

Rafiki Knows the Past Can Hurt—Precedent Doesn't Define Destiny

Every leader carries scars, some personal, some inherited from team culture. This chapter explores the emotional and organizational cost of unaddressed precedent and offers a servant leadership lens for healing. Learn how to reframe failure, name cultural wounds, and lead forward with courage, identity, and purpose.

There's a scene in *The Lion King* that's more than just Disney magic; it's a masterclass in emotional intelligence and leadership transformation.

Simba, broken and haunted by his past, avoids stepping into his rightful place. He's consumed by guilt, self-doubt, and fear of failure. That's when Rafiki the wise, slightly unhinged mandrill, whacks him on the head.

Startled, Simba says, "What was that for?"

Rafiki shrugs and says:

"It doesn't matter. It's in the past."

Simba retorts, "Yeah, but it still hurts."

And Rafiki without missing a beat says something every servant leader should tattoo on their heart:

"Oh yes, the past can hurt. But the way I see it, you can either run from it … or learn from it."

Mic drop.
Mandrill wisdom.
Leadership gold.

This chapter is about understanding the powerful tension between precedent and potential. It's about why servant leaders *must* confront their past, but not be confined by it. Because no matter what you've been through, or what culture you inherited, or what mistakes were made:

Your past doesn't define your future.
Your precedent doesn't limit your possibility.

The Leadership Trap: "This Is Just the Way It Is"

One of the most dangerous sentences in any organization is:

"That's how we've always done it."

It's subtle. It sounds harmless. But that phrase is often a death sentence for innovation, growth, and healing.

Precedent creates patterns. Some are helpful like standard protocols or brand consistency. But others become *anchors*, pulling us backward:

- Toxic culture we've normalized.
- Systems built on outdated needs.
- Leadership habits formed in survival mode.
- Internal scripts that say: "I'm not ready," or "I don't belong."

These patterns are powerful. But here's the truth:

Your brain was wired by your past.
But it can be rewired by your future.

That's the job of a servant leader: to face history honestly but refuse to be defined by it.

Past ≠ Identity

Too many leaders carry internal shame or hesitation that stems from the past:

- A failed project they still regret.
- A toxic boss they once emulated.
- A season of burnout they're still recovering from.
- A personal insecurity they've never named.

The danger isn't in having a past. We *all* have one.
The danger is in allowing that past to become identity.

"I failed at leading that change, so I'm not strategic."
"I was once an underperformer, so I shouldn't lead others."
"I lost my cool once. I'm not cut out for leadership."
"No one trusted me before. Why would they now?"

These narratives quietly sculpt ceilings over people's potential.
Servant leaders don't ignore these stories but they reframe them.

They choose to learn instead of hide.
To grow instead of grip.
To lead forward instead of limping backward.

When the Team Carries Scars

It's not just individuals who carry the past teams do too.

Maybe you've inherited a team where:

- Past leadership created fear and mistrust.
- Dysfunction was the norm.
- People were overworked and underheard.
- Mistakes were punished instead of processed.

This isn't rare as *Harvard Business Review* reports that 58 percent of employees trust a stranger more than their own boss after enduring toxic leadership. That's not just a trust problem; it's a cultural injury.

You might walk into that situation with a plan and a servant's heart, but the shadows still live in the culture.

You can feel it in the tension during meetings.
In the guarded responses.
In the silence where there should be collaboration.

As Rafiki says: *Oh yes, the past can hurt.*
But here's what servant leadership says in return:
"Yes, that happened. But we're not there anymore."

You don't have to pretend that the pain didn't exist. In fact, you shouldn't.
Healing starts with *naming what was*, so you can build what *will be*.

Great cultures are not built by accident.
They're crafted often in the fires of hard conversations, honest reflections, and courageous ownership.

And here's a paradox:
Sometimes the most powerful act of leadership isn't casting
a new vision, it's stopping long enough to ask:

What pain are we still carrying that's shaping how we work?
The answer might surprise you.

Maybe it's the fear of failure that came from a public firing.
Maybe it's the exhaustion of working under leaders who praised numbers but ignored people.
Maybe it's a history of promises broken, which is why your team greets your enthusiasm with cautious silence.
In these moments, don't rush to prove that you're different. Show it by leading differently.

How?

- Hold space for your team to share what's real, not just what's polite.
- Admit what wasn't okay. Even if you weren't there when it happened.
- Invite their stories, not just their performance.
- Ask, "What do you need from me to rebuild trust?" and *listen*.

Healing isn't a soft skill.
It's a business strategy.
Because the more whole your people are, the more fully they show up for each other, for your clients, and for the mission.

The Servant Leader's Path: From Scar to Mufasa

Let's get metaphorical for a moment.

There are two types of leadership legacies in *The Lion King*:

- Scar: Hoards power, leads through fear, blames others, and uses the past to manipulate.
- Mufasa: Dignifies others, teaches through example, and uses the past to *shape character*.

Every leader has Scar moments. We've all led poorly at some point. That doesn't disqualify us, it invites us to become better.

Servant leaders don't avoid the past.
They face it and then *transform* it.

Like Mufasa's voice in the sky said to Simba:
"You are more than what you have become."

What if you started saying that to yourself?
To your team?
To your culture?

What if you began leading with the belief that growth is always possible, even if pain came first?

The Cost of Carrying What No Longer Serves You

There's something subtle but corrosive that happens when we don't let go of the past:
We start carrying it into every decision we make.

It's like walking through today's challenges with yesterday's bruises still dictating our reflexes.
That one time someone dismissed your idea in a meeting?

Now you hesitate to speak up.
The project that bombed because you trusted the wrong person?
Now you do everything yourself, even when it burns you out.

What starts as protection becomes limitation.
And servant leaders cannot lead from fear-based patterns,
at least not for long.

Here's the truth:
Carrying what no longer serves you isn't strength.
It's spiritual clutter.
It's emotional weight that was meant to be acknowledged,
not permanently worn.

Simba's journey wasn't just about going home.
It was about shedding the shame, self-doubt, and false
beliefs that whispered:
"You're not enough."
"You're not ready."
"You don't deserve this."

Rafiki didn't magically fix Simba. He just disrupted the cycle.
He delivered a jolt physical and philosophical that reminded him:
You can either carry the past … or carry your purpose.
But you can't do both well.

Leadership Amnesia Versus Leadership Wisdom

There's a temptation in leadership to forget the past entirely.
To bulldoze ahead in the name of "fresh starts" and "new vision."
It sounds healthy, even inspiring.
But let's be clear: ignoring the past isn't healing its avoidance.
Leaders often fall into one of two traps:

1. **Leadership Amnesia**
   Where we pretend the hurt never happened.

Where we overwrite history with spin and silence, thinking time alone will heal.
It doesn't. It festers.

Or,

2. **Leadership Repetition**
   Where we unknowingly repeat the very behaviors that we hated.
   Micromanaging because we once felt out of control.
   Avoiding hard conversations because we are once weaponized truth.
   Hoarding decisions because trust was once broken.

Neither of these approaches honors the servant leader's calling.
What does?

Leadership Wisdom

Wisdom remembers the past but doesn't reenact it.
Wisdom mines pain for insight not identity.
Wisdom learns where the bruises are so we can
stop bumping into the same walls.

This is the essence of servant leadership:
We don't ignore the wounds.
We listen to them, learn from them, and then
lead from the scar not the scab.

The Shame No One Sees

There's a kind of shame most leaders don't talk about.
It's not always explosive. It's not a meltdown moment.
It's quieter. Internal. Lingering.

It's the shame of being imperfect in a role where you're expected to have answers.
It's the shame of your "leadership lowlights" playing louder than your wins.
It's the gnawing feeling that maybe ... you're not really who people think you are.

This kind of shame makes us reactive instead of reflective.
It makes us defensive instead of curious.
It makes us protect our image instead of developing our soul.

So how do servant leaders move through it?
By practicing something rare in corporate cultures:

Grace

Grace doesn't ignore accountability.
It invites accountability to grow *you*, not destroy you.
Grace says:

- "You got that wrong, but you are still right for this work."
- "You missed the mark, but you're learning how to aim better."
- "You're not your worst moment, you're what you choose next."

Every servant leader needs to lead themselves with the same empathy they give others.
Because transformation begins inward.

The Simba Moment: When Someone Reminds You Who You Are

Every servant leader has a moment sometimes more than one when they want to run.

From the pain.
From the pressure.
From the past.

But the world doesn't need more leaders running.
It needs more leaders *remembering.*

That's what Mufasa did for Simba.
He didn't give him a to-do list or a quarterly strategy.
He gave him identity.

He reminded him of something powerful:
"You are more than what you have become."

What if every leader had someone whispering that over them?
What if *you* became that voice for someone else?

What if instead of saying, "Why are you like this?"
You said, "This isn't all of who you are."

Practices for Healing and Hope

Here are practical ways servant leaders help themselves and their teams heal from and move beyond precedent.

1. **Name the Narrative**
   Ask yourself:
   - What stories from the past still play in your mind?
   - What beliefs do you hold about yourself because of failure, hurt, or history?
   - Where might you be operating from protection, not potential?

   Write those narratives down. Saying them aloud or putting them on paper disarms their power.
2. **Reframe the Experience**
   For every painful or limiting story, ask:
   - What did I learn?
   - How has it made me more empathetic or aware?
   - How could this be a strength in disguise?

   Pain doesn't disappear when it's reframed, but it becomes useful.
3. **Acknowledge Cultural Wounds**
   If you're leading a team with past trauma (toxic leadership, layoffs, favoritism), *name it* in a safe and humble way.

   Try this:

   "I know this team's been through a lot. I know things haven't always been healthy. But I'm here now to help us move forward together. It starts with listening and rebuilding trust."

   That kind of honesty wins hearts and according to Gallup, it also wins commitment. Employees who strongly agree that their leaders are transparent are 8.4 times more likely to be engaged in their work.

4. **Create Forward Rituals**

   Instead of just "moving on," servant leaders create rituals of forward momentum:

   - A postmortem after hard seasons or transitions.
   - A team reset conversation to redefine culture.
   - Celebrating the *firsts* of new ways: the first time someone speaks up, the first time a team member owns a project, and so on.

5. **Speak Future Identity**

   You don't just lead people where they are.

   You lead them into who they're becoming.

   Use identity-driven language:

   - "You're the kind of person who brings calm to the chaos."
   - "Our team is becoming one that others look to for solutions."
   - "This culture is changing, and you're a big part of why."

   That's Rafiki-style vision casting.

A Leadership Story: The New Simba

A leader I worked with inherited a veterinary clinic that had been through the wringer high turnover, broken trust, micromanagement. When she arrived, she was hopeful but quickly overwhelmed.

Everything she tried was met with suspicion or silence.

So she changed tactics.

She stopped trying to "fix" the past.

She started naming it.

At a team meeting, she said:

"I know leadership hasn't always been healthy here. I know some of you have been burned or unheard. I'm not here to pretend that didn't happen. I'm here to create something better and I need your help."

Something shifted. Walls lowered. Over time, the team healed. The culture evolved.

All because a leader chose to face the past, but *not be defined by it.*

Final Thoughts: The Future Is Still Yours

You're not stuck.

Not in your patterns.
Not in your past.
Not in the pain of what was.

Rafiki was right. The past *can* hurt.

But the hurt isn't the end. It's the *beginning* of transformation.

As a servant leader, you carry the torch of possibility. And your job isn't to erase the past—it's to build something better because of it.

"You can either run from it … or learn from it."

Choose to learn.
Choose to grow.
Choose to lead forward.

Because your precedent doesn't define your destiny.
But your perspective? That just might.

Simba didn't become king by forgetting the past; he became king by facing it.
You don't need to erase the scars. You just need to remember who you are.

Reflective Exercise: Rewriting the Leadership Story

1. **What personal or professional failure do you still carry?**
Describe the moment or season briefly. How did it make you feel? What identity did it try to give you?
2. **What is a limiting belief that came from that experience?**
Examples: I'm not strategic. I shouldn't speak up. I'm not trusted.
3. **Now reframe it. What did you learn? What strength came from it?**
Write a new identity statement. Example: That experience taught me to listen better. I now lead with empathy and depth.

4. **Think about your team's culture, what part of its past needs healing?**
   What pain or precedent might still be shaping how people work, speak, or trust?
5. **What's one message you can deliver that acknowledges the past while pointing forward?**
   Write it out as if you're saying it at your next team meeting.

"Remember who you are."—*Mufasa*

Because when you do, the past loses its grip and your leadership comes alive.

PART II

Owning Your Voice and Actions

CHAPTER 5

Take Advice From Ludacris—Act a Fool

Leadership doesn't have to be rigid to be respected. This chapter explores how playful, vulnerable, and even foolish moments can unlock connection, creativity, and trust. In times of stress or disconnection, a little levity can go a long way. Because the leaders people remember aren't always the ones who play it safe, they're the ones who show up fully human.

"If you gon' act a fool, act a fool."—*Ludacris*

You probably didn't expect to find a leadership lesson in a 2003 hip-hop anthem featured in *2 Fast 2 Furious*. But bear with me.

Because sometimes, the best way to lead is to act a little foolish intentionally, strategically, and unapologetically.

Not foolish as in reckless.
Not foolish as in incompetent.
But foolish as in *free*.

This chapter is about authenticity, playfulness, and taking yourself less seriously even (and especially) in leadership. Because the weight of leadership can crush you if you forget to bring levity, humanity, and some well-timed foolishness to the table.

Servant leadership isn't just about humility and service.
It's also about *permission* to be real, to be goofy, and to break the mold.

In fact, sometimes the most profound leadership move is to *disarm the room* with laughter, vulnerability, and a little unexpected foolishness.

What "Acting a Fool" Really Means

Let's redefine the term.

"Acting a fool" in servant leadership means:

- Breaking tension with humor.
- Showing personality instead of polish.
- Dancing when the room needs a rhythm reset.
- Laughing at yourself so others can breathe.
- Saying what everyone's thinking but with compassion and style.

It's the opposite of sterile professionalism. It's what breathes *life* into a culture.

When Ludacris said "act a fool," he was talking about turning the volume up on life doing something bold, loud, maybe even absurd. And while you don't need to peel out in a muscle car in the clinic parking lot (unless, of course, that's your thing), you *do* need to ask:

Have I become too buttoned-up to be believable?

Because authenticity *connects*, and sometimes the most authentic leaders are the ones unafraid to be a little silly.

The Problem With Overprofessionalism

Somewhere along the way, many leaders were taught that "professional" meant:

- Emotionless
- Perfectly composed
- Always polished
- No visible weakness
- No humor unless preapproved

But let me ask you this:

- When was the last time you *connected* with someone because they were perfect?

- When was the last time you trusted a person who never cracked a smile?
- When was the last time a moment of ridiculous laughter didn't lift a room?

Exactly.

Over-polished leaders often create sterile environments. And sterile environments are *brittle*. They crack under pressure. They repel creativity. They silence authenticity.

The antidote?

Let yourself be a *little foolish*.

Servant Leadership Is Human-First, Not Image-First

When you lead from the bottom-up inverted you prioritize people, not optics. That means:

- You laugh when it's funny.
- You admit when you don't know.
- You make the dumb pun even if no one laughs.
- You wear the costume on Spirit Day.
- You dance awkwardly during the staff party and own it.

This doesn't diminish your credibility, it *builds it.*

Because people trust *real* leaders. Leaders who aren't afraid to be both passionate and playful. Competent and clownish (on occasion). Bold and unfiltered (within reason).

The leader who can walk into the breakroom and act out a bad Yelp review just to make the team laugh; that's the leader people want to follow.

What Acting a Fool Looks Like in Practice

Here's how "strategic foolishness" shows up in real-world servant leadership:

1. **Use Humor to De-escalate**

   Tension in the room? Team on edge? Inject some levity.

"We're not curing cancer we're just trying to get Mr. Pickles the cat to take his meds without biting off Lisa's hand."

Humor breaks the spiral. It clears the air.

2. **Make Fun of Yourself—First**

   Your title doesn't protect you from mistakes. So why pretend?

   "Don't follow my example from last Thursday. I created a scheduling vortex that disrupted space and time."

   Humility with a laugh builds safety.

3. **Celebrate With Ridiculous Rituals**

   Silly rituals build team identity.

   - Ring a cowbell when someone hits a milestone.
   - Have a trophy named "The Golden Syringe" for funniest tech fail.
   - Do a "victory dance" every time the schedule actually holds.

   It doesn't matter what it is; it matters that it's *yours*.

4. **Give Out Awards That Mean Nothing (But Everything)**

   Make up awards that are meaningless in form but meaningful in fun:

   - "Fastest Drawer Opener."
   - "Best Accidental Double-Booked Appointment Recovery."
   - "Most Coffee Consumed Without Crying."

   When you laugh with your team, you build *belonging*.

5. **Use Music and Movement**

   Create a Spotify playlist for "clinic vibes." Let the team DJ on Fridays. If it's a chaotic day, pause and dance it out for 60 seconds. Yes really.

   Foolish? Maybe. Effective? Absolutely.

A Story: The Halloween Costume That Changed a Clinic

A clinic manager I coached was known for being competent, steady, and professional—but distant. Her team respected her but didn't *love* her.

Then came Halloween.

She showed up dressed as a six-foot-tall flea. She leaned into it. Did rounds in character. Made jokes about "jumping" between departments.

The team *lost it*. The walls dropped. Something shifted.

From that moment forward, they saw her differently not just as a leader, but as a *person*. Engagement rose. Morale spiked. And people started suggesting their own ways to "act a fool" together theme days, inside jokes, silly awards.

All because one leader decided to stop being the safest version of herself.

Acting a Fool in Hard Times: Leading With Light When the Room Is Heavy

It's easy to act a fool when things are going well.
When the energy is high, the schedule is smooth, and no
one is crying in the supply closet, humor comes easy.

But the real test?
Can you still bring levity when the room is tense?
Can you still offer playfulness when the stakes are high?
Can you still show up as your full, foolish self
when the team is running on fumes?

That's the deeper magic of servant leadership.
Because the power of "acting a fool" isn't in how loud or flashy it is.
It's in how well-timed it is.

Strategic foolishness is courage in disguise.

Why Humor Feels Risky but Matters Most

Humor is vulnerable.
It's putting yourself out there.
It's risking a joke that falls flat.
It's doing the unexpected when people expect you to be "serious."

But that's exactly what makes it powerful.

A 2021 Gallup Workplace study found that teams with high psychological safety where members feel comfortable showing vulnerability are 27 percent more likely to report excellent performance and 50 percent more likely to retain top talent. Humor and lightheartedness are key indicators of that safety.

Because tension thrives in silence.
It loves when people stay guarded.
It grows when leaders are distant, polished, and emotionally armored.

Humor disrupts that cycle.

When a leader laughs even in chaos it signals something profound:
We are still human here.
We are still allowed to feel joy.
We are not defined by this hard season.

That kind of leadership?
It's unforgettable.

Foolishness as Emotional Oxygen

You know what a clinic smells like when stress has been sitting too long? Stale.

Same with culture.

When people haven't laughed in weeks, the air gets heavy.
It's harder to breathe creatively, emotionally, and relationally.

A Mayo Clinic review found that laughter not only reduces stress hormones like cortisol but also increases immune-boosting cells and infection-fighting antibodies, improving overall resistance to disease.

Foolishness acts like a cultural oxygen mask.
It says: "Breathe. We're still here. We're still together."

You don't need to solve all the problems in the room to lighten the air.
You just need to let yourself be a little ridiculous.

Not to distract from reality but to remind people that they're more than what they're going through.

"But What If They Don't Take Me Seriously?"

Ah yes. The common fear of many high-achieving, high-responsibility leaders.

Here's a reframe:

They won't take you seriously **if they can't feel you**.

If you're always buttoned up and behind a desk emotionally or physically, people respect your position, but not always your person.

The leader who walks the floor in a banana costume to celebrate hitting a monthly goal?
That's someone people follow because they trust them.
Because they know:

- "You see me."
- "You're one of us."
- "You care enough to let go of the image."

Respect isn't built on constant seriousness.
It's built on **consistency, courage, and connection**.

And connection often starts with laughter.

When Laughter Is Leadership

Let's be clear: humor doesn't replace accountability.
It doesn't fix burnout or cover up dysfunction.
It's not about being the "fun boss" who avoids hard conversations.

True servant leaders know that levity without honesty is just noise.

But when laughter is paired with clarity and care?
It becomes leadership.

It becomes a bridge between "I see you" and "We'll get through this."
It becomes a balm for tired teams.
It becomes a culture signal that says:

"We're allowed to enjoy this work even when it's hard."

Story: When the ER Was Falling Apart

I once worked with a veterinary ER that hit a brutal season short-staffed, emotionally drained, constantly in triage mode. The team was functioning, but just barely.

The medical director, a brilliant, no-nonsense clinician, did something unexpected one Friday night.

She rolled into the breakroom with a karaoke machine and belted out Whitney Houston's "I Wanna Dance with Somebody" with zero shame and a lot of off-key passion.

No announcement. No buildup. Just joy.

For a moment, everything stopped.
People laughed. Some cried. A few joined in.

No one was fixed. The chaos didn't disappear.
But something shifted.

She reminded them that they weren't machines.
That leadership could be strong and silly.
That fun wasn't something to "earn" it was something to protect.

Morale didn't turn around overnight. But from that day, the room felt different.

That's leadership. That's acting a fool with purpose.

Practical Foolishness: Go-To Moves for Heavy Seasons

When things feel heavy, consider these low effort, high-impact ways to bring light:

1. **Dramatic Weather Reports**
   Start your staff huddle with a "forecast" of the day, delivered like a news anchor.

"Today's outlook includes a 70 percent chance of double-bookings and a 100 percent chance of caffeine dependency."

2. **Themed Snack Days**
   Make Mondays "Muffin Mood Check" days. You bring muffins, the team rates the day on a muffin scale.
3. **Unexpected Compliments**
   Handwrite ridiculous but oddly specific affirmations:
   "You document with the grace of a caffeinated gazelle."
   "Your IV skills could probably save a raccoon in zero gravity."
4. **Group Photo Challenges**
   Pick a theme "Most Dramatic Glove Removal" or "Best Pretend Phone Call with a Difficult Client."
   Photos only. Laughter guaranteed.
5. **Out-of-Context Quote Boards**
   Write down the funniest out-of-context quote from the day. Example: "If the ferret wears the cone, I'm quitting."

Don't Wait for the Culture to Change; Be the Culture Disruptor

Too many leaders wait for "better morale" before introducing humor. But that's backward.

Morale Doesn't Improve Without Someone Taking the First Foolish Step

Someone must model what joy looks like.
Someone must risk looking silly to make others feel safe.

That someone is you.
You have more influence than you think.

Your tone sets the tone.
Your permission grants permission.
Your foolishness creates freedom.

The Deeper Risk of Playing It Too Safe

The real danger in leadership isn't being foolish.
It's being **forgettable**.

It's leading so safely that no one connects.
It's protecting your image so fiercely that no one sees your heart.
It's believing that credibility only comes in a suit and not in a smile.

So go ahead:

- Wear the costume.
- Make the playlist.
- Print the meme.
- Laugh loudly.
- Dance terribly.
- Joke kindly.
- Lead playfully.

Because when you act a fool with intention, you don't lose respect; you build belonging.

And in a world that asks leaders to do more and feel less?

That's the bravest kind of leadership there is.

What "Foolish" Actually Teaches

Foolishness teaches:

- Psychological safety (it's safe to be yourself here).
- Permission to play (we're not just task robots).
- Emotional balance (it's okay to laugh even when things are hard).
- Trust through authenticity (you don't need a mask to matter).

It also teaches leaders something critical:
You don't have to be heavy to be taken seriously.

Reflection: Are You Playing Too Small?

Ask yourself:

- When was the last time I laughed *with* my team not just around them?
- Have I made professionalism a barrier to connection?
- What would it look like to "act a fool" in a way that's true to me?

Because let's be honest; if you've forgotten how to have fun, you've forgotten how to lead *people*.

Final Thoughts: Own the Room, Then Loosen It Up

Inverted leadership isn't about pretending to be something you're not; it's about being *more fully* who you are in service of others.

Sometimes that means guiding.
Sometimes that means protecting.
And sometimes, it means acting a fool.

So, dance at the all-hands-on-deck meeting.
Tell the dumb joke in the morning huddle.
Make a meme about your own leadership quirks.

So, when the work feels too heavy, the room is too quiet, or your people too distant, channel your inner Ludacris.

Act a fool. On purpose. With love. And for the culture you want to create.

And when people ask why?
Just tell them:
"Ludacris told me to."

Reflective Exercise: Find Your Fool

Take 10–15 minutes to answer the following:

1. **Where have I been "too professional" at the expense of authenticity?**
   List two to three situations where you played it too safe or held back your personality.
2. **What's one silly thing I used to do that made others laugh or smile?**
   Could be from a past job, childhood, or a forgotten leadership moment.
3. **What's one way I can "act a fool" in the next week?**
   It could be small—a pun, a costume, a joke, or a goofy walk. The goal is lightness, not perfection.
4. **What would it look like if my team knew they could laugh *with* me, not just around me?**
   Describe that version of your team.
5. **Write your fool statement:**
   "I give myself permission to be real, light, and joyful in my leadership. Because my people deserve a leader who's fully human, not just fully polished."

"The most wasted of all days is one without laughter."

—*E. E. Cummings*

And the most disconnected of all leaders is the one who forgets how.

So lead smart. Lead strong.
But every now and then
Act a fool.

CHAPTER 6

You've Got Mail—Own Every Message You Send

In leadership, communication isn't about what's said, it's about what's received. This chapter explores how intentional message delivery builds culture, connection, and clarity. Because leadership doesn't just speak, it delivers meaning.

At some point in every leader's journey, there comes a moment of reckoning.
You walk into the breakroom and feel the tension before anyone speaks.
You send an e-mail you thought was clear, and five different people interpret it five different ways.
You give feedback with good intent and someone leaves that conversation feeling wounded.

What happened?

You delivered the message.
But you didn't deliver it well.

Leadership isn't just about speaking; it's about being responsible for what's actually received.

Think of yourself like the mail carrier of your culture. Every interaction, every update, and every coaching moment is a delivery. And with every delivery, you have a choice:

- Will this message build trust or erode it?
- Will it inspire clarity or create confusion?
- Will it reflect your values or just your authority?

As a servant leader, you don't just deliver messages; you deliver meaning. And meaning is your responsibility.

Mail Metaphor 101: Delivering Is More Than Dropping

Let's take a simple truth from the US Postal Service:

The job isn't just to *drop off the mail*; it's to make sure it gets where it needs to go, in the right condition, to the right person.

Now let's apply that to leadership.

It's not enough to:

- Post an update to Slack and call it communication.
- Leave a sticky note with feedback and walk away.
- Mention a policy change in passing and expect buy-in.

That's dropping mail.

Not delivering it.

Delivery means:

- Ensuring that your message is clear.
- Making sure the *right people* understand it.
- Anticipating how it will land.
- Following up to confirm that it was received *with the meaning you intended.*

Inverted leadership flips the script. It says:

"I'm responsible for what I say *and* how it's received."

Because when a message misses, it's not just a dropped ball; it's a dropped connection. In fact, a study by the Economist Intelligence Unit found that poor workplace communication leads to project delays or failures for 44 percent of employees and costs companies an average of $62.4 million per year in lost productivity.

Good Leaders Communicate. Great Leaders Confirm.

Here's a common leadership myth:

"I said it, so I communicated it."

Nope.

Saying something doesn't guarantee communication.

Communication isn't what leaves your mouth.

It's what enters their mind and heart with clarity and purpose.

That's the difference between broadcasting and delivering.

- Broadcasting pushes information outward, without checking for understanding.
- Delivering means tailoring, timing, and following through with context and care.

Your message isn't delivered until it's understood. Gallup research shows that employees who strongly agree that their manager communicates clearly are 73 percent more engaged at work and engagement is directly linked to higher productivity, lower turnover, and stronger customer satisfaction.

What You *Always* Deliver (Whether You Mean To or Not)

Even when you're not speaking, you're delivering messages. Your presence, your body language, your silence, your priorities, they all say something.

Here are some unintentional messages that leaders deliver:

- Ignoring someone's question: "You don't matter."
- Canceling 1:1s repeatedly: "I don't have time for you."
- Praising only the loudest team members: "Only extroverts win here."
- Rolling your eyes in a meeting: "This isn't a safe space to speak up."
- Never giving feedback: "There's no growth here."

You're delivering culture whether you mean to or not.

So ask: What am I sending out into the world, even when I'm not talking?

When Delivery Fails

Let's look at a few common failures in message delivery and what they cost.

1. **The "Drive-by Directive"**
   You rush in, give an instruction, and rush out. You think you've been clear. The team is left blinking and confused.
   Impact: Frustration, misalignment, mistakes.
   Solution: Slow down. Frame the "why." Ask for confirmation.
2. **The "Assumed Understanding"**
   You've explained something once. You assume that everyone gets it. They don't.
   Impact: Inconsistent behavior, resentment, blame.
   Solution: Repeat with empathy. Ask, "What does this look like to you in action?"
3. **The "Emotional Baggage Drop"**
   You're frustrated. You say what's on your mind. The team gets the message, but also gets your stress, tone, and tension.
   Impact: Fear, disengagement, emotional shutdown.
   Solution: Pause. Process your emotion *before* delivery.
4. **The "Silent Delivery"**
   You think, "They should know this by now." So you don't say anything. No feedback, no recognition, no direction.
   Impact: Assumptions, drifting standards, invisible efforts.
   Solution: Say what needs to be said. Silence is also a message and usually not a good one.

The Servant Leader's Delivery Checklist

Before you "drop the mail," ask yourself:

1. Is the message clear?
   Would I understand this if I were on the receiving end?

2. Is the tone aligned with the intent?
   Am I being calm, respectful, and constructive?
3. Is this the right time and setting?
   Am I delivering this in a moment when it can be heard and processed?
4. Have I considered their perspective?
   How might this message land, based on what they're going through?
5. Have I followed up?
   Did I circle back to make sure they *received* the message, not just heard the words?

The Message You Never Meant to Send

Not every message we send is the one we *meant* to send. And as leaders, we often forget that silence, inconsistency, or a poorly timed phrase can deliver more than a dozen well-crafted e-mails.

A technician once told me, "It's not the policy that hurt. It's how I found out about it, tacked to the wall like a flyer for a lost cat."

That leader didn't mean to be dismissive. They were probably busy, overwhelmed, and moving fast. But intention doesn't excuse impact.

In today's world, where burnout is high and trust can be low, it's not enough to have the right messages we have to deliver them with presence.

Presence isn't about perfection. It's about care. Being aware enough to know:

- When your tone adds weight instead of clarity.
- When your timing prevents people from hearing what you're saying.
- When your stress is leaking into your message.
- When your nonverbal communication is louder than your actual words.

Inverted leaders don't just ask, "What am I saying?"
They ask, "What are they hearing?"

Let's get practical.

Missed Message #1: The "Neutral" Update

You send a well-worded e-mail announcing a schedule change. It's neutral, efficient, and professional.

You think: "This is clear."
They feel: "We weren't consulted."
What's missing: Connection and context. People want to feel informed *and* included. Even a simple, "We know this may be a disruption, and we're here to support you through it," can change the entire tone.

Missed Message #2: The Performance Sandwich

You offer praise, slip in some critical feedback, and then wrap with more praise. You're trying to be kind.
But they walk away confused or worse, only hearing the negative.

The message: "I don't know if I'm doing well or failing."
What's missing: Clarity. Don't hide your message. Deliver it with empathy, not padding.

Missed Message #3: The Delayed Response

You wait to give feedback until the moment passes. Maybe you're trying to avoid conflict. Maybe you're just exhausted. Either way, what they hear is:
"I guess it didn't matter."
What's missing: Timeliness. Delayed feedback is diluted feedback.

So What Do You Do Instead?

Great leaders don't just deliver what's convenient to say.
They deliver what's needed with clarity, consistency, and emotional intelligence.

Here's a framework you can use before you hit send, speak up, or stay silent:

The 3P Filter:

1. **Purpose**—What is the actual reason for this message?
2. **People**—How will this land with the person or team receiving it?
3. **Presence**—Am I showing up with awareness, not just words?

Let's say you're announcing a new process.

- Purpose: To create clarity and reduce mistakes.
- People: Some will welcome the clarity. Others might fear they're being micromanaged.
- Presence: Acknowledge the human response first, then explain the "why," and invite questions.

Suddenly, it's not a message it's a conversation.

Real Story: The Message That Changed a Culture

A new hospital director walked into a struggling team. Turnover was high. Trust was low. Everyone felt overlooked and exhausted.

She started each day with the same phrase:

"Let's make today a better story."

Then, she backed it up by:

- Delivering feedback with care and context.
- Celebrating small wins loudly and specifically.
- Having tough conversations privately, with empathy.
- Writing handwritten notes after hard days.
- Repeating the vision again and again and again.

Over six months, the culture shifted.

Not because of a new policy.
Not because of a flashy strategy.
But because she owned what she delivered—every day.

Message Delivery = Culture Building

You don't need a culture initiative to shape culture.
You just need to own your daily deliveries.

Think about it:

- Every time you give feedback, you're building psychological safety or shrinking it.
- Every time you cast vision, you're creating clarity or confusion.
- Every time you respond to a mistake, you're modeling growth or shame.

Every moment is mail.
And inverted leadership means choosing to deliver trust, clarity, and compassion on repeat.

You don't just lead the team.
You deliver the heartbeat of the culture, one message at a time.

Reflective Exercise: The Mail You're Delivering

Take 15 minutes to reflect:

1. **What's the last message you delivered that landed poorly?**
   What could you have done differently in your tone, timing, or follow-up?
2. **Think of a time someone misunderstood your intention.**
   What message did they hear, and what did you actually mean?
3. **What messages do you deliver consistently without words?**
   Consider your habits, expressions, priorities, and presence.
4. **Who on your team needs a message of encouragement or clarity this week?**
   Write what you'll say and how you'll say it.
5. **Write your leadership delivery statement:**
   "I own what I say and how it's received. I will lead with clarity, empathy, and follow-through. Because every message I deliver shapes the culture I'm responsible for."

Final Thoughts: Deliver With Integrity, Lead With Intent

It's easy to think your job is just to pass along updates or set direction. But inverted leadership says otherwise:

You don't just pass the message.
You embody it.
You don't just speak with clarity.
You lead with consistency.
You don't just "check the box" on communication.
You build connection through delivery.

So take the time. Shape the message. Own the tone.
Because you're not just delivering mail, you're delivering meaning.

CHAPTER 7

Santa, the Easter Bunny, the Tooth Fairy, and the Wizard: Letting Go of Leadership Myths

This chapter challenges the common leadership myths we grow up believing like the Santa Claus CEO or the Wizard in the tower and reveals how they shape disengaged, dependent teams. Through vivid metaphors and real-world examples, we explore four archetypes of "mythical leadership": the Santa Claus (the fixer), the Easter Bunny (the celebrator who avoids conflict), the Tooth Fairy (the soother who distracts), and the Wizard (the distant strategist). Each represents well-intentioned but ultimately disconnected leadership. In contrast, servant leadership is about presence over pageantry showing up consistently, communicating transparently, and empowering others to lead. Practical strategies and reflection exercises help leaders move from mythical to meaningful, trading heroism for humanity. Because real leadership isn't about magic, it's about being there when it matters most.

When I was a kid, I believed in Santa Claus. I believed in the Easter Bunny, the Tooth Fairy, and Wizards too. They were magical, comforting figures showing up in the middle of the night with gifts, candy, or a dollar under the pillow, asking for nothing in return. But, of course, that wasn't the truth. The truth was even better: it was my parents. They did the work; quietly, faithfully, usually late at night after long days because they loved me.

They didn't wear red suits, hop around with baskets, fly through windows, or cast magical spells. They showed up tired, consistent, flawed, and still giving. That's real leadership.

The Illusion of the Hero Leader

In many businesses, we inherit myths not unlike the ones we held as children. We believe in the charismatic CEO who can fix any problem. We put faith in leaders who "always have the answer." We rely on quarterly performance speeches like we once waited for the jingle of sleigh bells. It's seductive. But it's dangerous.

Why? Because it detaches leadership from reality. It builds a culture where employees wait to be saved instead of being empowered. Where people look up for answers instead of within themselves or across their teams. In fact, Gallup's 2023 *State of the Global Workplace* report found that only 21 percent of employees are engaged at work globally, with poor leadership communication cited as a major driver. Hero-leader myths don't just waste potential; they actively contribute to this disengagement.

These myths—let's call them "business folklore"—encourage the idea that the leader is the one with the magic: the vision, the charm, the big decisions. Everyone else just executes. That's not leadership. That's pageantry.

A servant leader doesn't hoard magic. They teach people how to create it for themselves. They don't perform; they partner. They don't sweep in once a year; they walk beside their team every day.

Let's break down what I call the three mythical leadership archetypes and how servant leadership inverts each one to build a business grounded in reality, empowerment, and positivity.

The Santa Claus Leader: The Fixer From the Sky

Santa shows up once a year. He keeps a list (which most leaders do), he drops off rewards, and then he disappears without conversation or explanation.

In business, this shows up in leaders who:

- Only engage during reviews, bonuses, or promotions.
- Suddenly appear to "fix" a problem with little understanding of the context.
- Make decisions behind closed doors, then present them as gifts.

It's leadership that feels magical until you realize that it's distant and disempowering.

Inversion Strategy: Be Available, Not Just Impressive

One of my most effective managers never walked into a room with fireworks. He wasn't loud. He didn't make sweeping pronouncements. But he was *always there* walking the floor, checking in, asking questions. Not to catch mistakes, but to understand the people doing the work.

Presence builds trust.

As a servant leader, stop thinking that your value is in the grand gestures. Instead, build a rhythm of visibility and approachability. Don't just show up when there's a gift to give. Show up when there's nothing to offer but your time, your listening, and your support.

The Easter Bunny Leader: The Celebrator Who Disappears

The Easter Bunny is a symbol of celebration and surprise colorful eggs hidden just out of sight. In organizations, this looks like the leader who shows up for team wins and big events but vanishes when things get hard.

We see this in leaders who:

- Appear only at product launches, holiday parties, or town halls.
- Disengage during team conflict, high stress, or failure.
- Avoid feedback loops unless it's time to give praise.

This breeds a culture of conditional visibility. Teams learn that the leader only appears when things are going well. Struggle, therefore, becomes a solitary experience.

Inversion Strategy: Be Present in the Mess

Here's something I learned the hard way: if you only walk into a room when it's decorated and clean, your team will hide the mess. That's not transparency. That's fear.

One of my team leads came to me once and said, "I almost didn't tell you we were behind, because I didn't want to disappoint you." That hit me like a brick. I thought I was creating a positive culture but what I was really doing was only showing up when things were polished.

Now, I make a point to ask questions like:

- What's not working?
- What do you need from me that you're not getting?
- Where are you stuck?

And then I stay. Even when the answers are uncomfortable. Especially then.

You earn the right to celebrate the highs by being present for the lows.

The Tooth Fairy Leader:
The Soother With a Payoff

The Tooth Fairy leaves money under your pillow for something you've lost. The business version of this is the leader who uses perks, distractions, or surface-level gestures to mask deeper issues.

Think:

- Pizza parties after layoffs.
- New tech toys instead of fair compensation.
- "Wellness Wednesdays" while people are burned out.

These are short-term strategies for long-term issues. And while the intention might be positive, the message received is often this: "We're uncomfortable with your discomfort, so here's something shiny."

Inversion Strategy: Honor the Loss, Lead Through It

Servant leadership doesn't avoid hard conversations; it dignifies them.

When you lose a key employee, when a team burns out, when you cancel a project, everyone believed in you don't throw a distraction. You name the pain. You grieve with the team. Then you point forward.

The truth is, people don't expect you to fix everything. They expect you to be *with them* through it.

As a leader, ask yourself:

- Am I trying to distract my team or support them?
- Have I created space for emotional processing, or just tried to move on?
- Have I *earned* the celebration I'm offering?

Sometimes the most powerful thing you can do is say: "This sucks. I'm here. Let's figure out what's next."

The Wizard Leader: The All-Knowing Oracle Behind the Curtain

There's one more mythical figure we need to talk about, the Wizard. Think Oz. Think Dumbledore. Think any leader perched high in a tower, wise and mysterious, casting strategy from behind closed doors. These leaders often aren't flashy or disconnected, they're revered. Quiet. Visionary. And a little intimidating.

In business, the Wizard Leader is often seen as:

- The strategic genius who doesn't involve themselves in day-to-day operations.
- The decision maker whose rationale is rarely shared with the team.
- The "brain" of the operation, separated from the "hands and feet."

This archetype isn't obviously toxic. In fact, many Wizard Leaders are admired by their teams. But the problem isn't admiration, it's access.

When you rely too heavily on your intelligence and vision without relational transparency, your team starts to operate in the dark. They don't see your thinking. They don't know your why. And they're too intimidated to ask.

You might hear things like:

- "I don't want to bother you with that."
- "I'm sure they've already thought about it."
- "They're probably too busy for my input."

That's not empowerment. That's silent hierarchy.

Inversion Strategy: Share the Blueprint

If you want your team to build the future with you, they have to understand how you think—not just what you want.

Here's a story: I once had a manager who'd come back from executive meetings with new directives and no context. "We're shifting priorities this quarter," he'd say. "Start with Project Blue." That was it. No backstory. No explanation. No invitation into the thought process. The team felt like pawns being moved on a board we couldn't see. Morale dropped. Engagement slipped. And resentment grew not because of the workload, but because of the opacity.

Eventually, we asked for insight. "Can you just tell us what's behind the shift?" And to his credit, he started to explain his process. He talked us through the market data, the executive discussions, and the customer feedback. Suddenly, we weren't just executors; we were insiders. It changed everything.

As a servant leader, your job isn't to be the smartest person in the room. It's to make sure that smart decisions are understood, trusted, and co-owned. That only happens when you invite people into your mental model.

Try these simple shifts:

- Instead of "Here's the decision," say: "Here's the decision and here's why we landed on it."
- Instead of "I've made a plan," say: "Here's the draft what am I missing?"
- Instead of hoarding vision, teach your team how to develop it with you.

Because true strategic brilliance isn't just seeing the future, it's helping others see it too.

From Archetypes to Authenticity

Let's pause for a moment.

You've now met the four mythical leadership archetypes:

1. **Santa Claus**—The once-a-year fixer.
2. **Easter Bunny**—The celebrator who avoids conflict.
3. **Tooth Fairy**—The soother who avoids depth.
4. **Wizard**—The visionary who withholds clarity.

All four come from a good place. Each one is rooted in some leadership strength rewarding, recognizing, protecting, and guiding. But when used in isolation or without self-awareness, they become masks. And masks create distance.

Authentic leadership requires unmasking. It requires you to:

- Be consistent, not occasional.
- Be honest, not performative.
- Be available, not just wise.
- Be human, not mythic.

That's the core of servant leadership: rejecting myth in favor of meaningful connection.

The Cost of Myth-Driven Leadership

If all of this sounds abstract, let's talk about the real cost of myth-driven leadership. Because it's not just about how people feel, it's about how businesses perform.

Mythical leadership cultures tend to produce:

- **High dependency**—Teams that wait to be told what to do.
- **Low resilience**—A workforce that cracks under pressure because the leader vanishes when things go wrong.
- **Surface loyalty**—People who smile at celebrations but disengage quietly.
- **Decision bottlenecks**—Because only the Wizard has the map, no one else can drive.

In contrast, teams led by servant leaders tend to be:

- **Empowered**—Because they've been taught how to think, not just what to do.
- **Resilient**—Because they've practiced honesty, even in the hard times.
- **Loyal**—Because trust isn't demanded; it's earned through consistency.
- **Distributed**—Because leadership is shared, not hoarded.

It's not just more human; it's more effective. Research supports this. A 2020 study in *The Leadership & Organization Development Journal* found that servant leadership behaviors correlated with a 6 to 13 percent increase in team productivity, alongside measurable gains in trust and collaboration. Humanity and performance, it turns out, aren't trade-offs; they reinforce each other.

What It Looks Like in Practice

Let me show you a quick contrast:

Mythical Leader	Servant Leader
Drops in to announce changes	Includes team in shaping the change
Recognizes wins, avoids struggles	Shows up consistently, even in failure
Distracts from discomfort	Names it and walks through it
Guards strategic thinking	Shares rationale and invites input
Leads from a pedestal	Leads from alongside

This isn't a personality shift. It's a posture shift.

And it's one that transforms not only culture but also results.

Final Reflection: Which Mask Am I Wearing?

Let's go deeper than surface self-assessment.

Ask yourself:

- When things get tough, do I become more visible or more removed?
- Do my team members understand *why* we're doing what we're doing?

- Have I ever accidentally created a persona that keeps people at arm's length?
- Do I lead in a way that builds future leaders or reinforces dependence on me?

Servant leadership isn't about being soft. It's about being strong enough to be vulnerable, available, and clear.

It's not about giving up authority. It's about giving away power.

And it's not about fixing everything for everyone. It's about being someone others want to build with especially when the magic wears off.

Real Leadership Is Uncomfortable and Worth It

Letting go of these myths doesn't mean letting go of inspiration. On the contrary, when people see a leader who is honest, consistent, and fully human, they start to believe that they can lead too.

Not because they're perfect.

But because they're *present.*

That's the power of inversion. Flipping the narrative from "I have to be the hero" to "I have to be here." From "I deliver value" to "I develop people." From "Look at me" to "I see you."

Practical Tools: From Myth to Method

Here are some ways you can start leading from presence, not myth:

1. **Weekly Vulnerability Check-Ins**
    - Ask your team: "What's one thing you're struggling with that I might not see?"
    - Share something you're personally working on, too.
2. **"See Me" Sessions**
    - Instead of performance reviews, schedule time just to understand your people. What motivates them? What blocks them? What are they proud of?
3. **Create Failure Rituals**
    - Instead of avoiding talk about failed projects, have a ritual to reflect, learn, and recognize the effort involved.

4. **Honor the Ordinary**
   - Don't wait for birthdays or big wins to show appreciation. Celebrate consistency. Celebrate the teammate who helped someone else shine.
5. **Don't Disappear**
   - During crises or organizational changes, we overcommunicate. Even if you don't have all the answers, presence breeds confidence.

Closing: From Magic to Meaning

As a kid, I believed in magic. As a leader, I believe in meaning.

Meaning is created not by distance and dazzle, but by connection and care. By telling your team the truth. By showing up. By walking with them not in front of them with sleeves rolled up and ears open.

So, leave the red suit at home.

Put down the glitter eggs.

Keep your dollar bills in your wallet.

Your team doesn't need a fantasy.

They need *you*; real, present, consistent, imperfect, and fully invested in helping them grow.

And that? That's more powerful than magic.

Reflection and Action: From Myth to Meaningful Leadership

Take a few minutes to reflect on the following questions. Write your thoughts down; don't just think them. Leadership growth happens when we move from theory to intention.

1. Which leadership myth do I most relate to: Santa, the Easter Bunny, or the Tooth Fairy?
   Be honest. When do I tend to disappear, overcompensate, or try to "save the day" instead of serve the team?
2. Where am I most present for my team right now?
   And where am I most *absent*?

3. What is one behavior I can change this week to move from reactive leadership to consistent presence?
   (Examples: Daily walk-throughs, a standing 1:1, sharing something personal in a team meeting.)
4. Who on my team might need me to show up differently?
   Think of one individual you've been distant from or have misunderstood. What's one action you can take to reconnect?
5. When was the last time I showed up without a solution just to listen? How did that go? What did I learn from it?

Next Step

Choose one insight from your reflection and commit to a small action this week. It doesn't have to be dramatic. Just intentional.

> Because leadership isn't about doing everything.
> It's about doing *one real thing*, consistently.

CHAPTER 8

No One Becomes Batman Without Falling Into the Cave

This chapter introduces the metaphor of the cave as the essential, often difficult space where true leadership is formed. Drawing on Batman's origin story, it explores how moments of fear, failure, and isolation are not signs of weakness but opportunities for transformation. Leaders learn to embrace these "cave moments" to build resilience, humility, and authenticity. The chapter also highlights how servant leaders navigate these challenges differently by leaning into vulnerability and connection, ultimately emerging stronger and more grounded to lead others effectively.

Introduction: The Cave as the Crucible of Leadership

In popular culture, Batman's origin story is iconic and for good reason. The defining moment is when young Bruce Wayne falls into a deep, dark cave beneath Wayne Manor. It's a moment of fear and vulnerability, but it's also the beginning of transformation.

This cave represents the trials every leader must face. It's not a physical space but a metaphorical one—a place of challenge, introspection, and growth.

No one steps into leadership fully formed and unscathed.
No one "arrives" at excellence without falling, sometimes hard.

If you want to lead like Batman resilient, purposeful, and unwavering, you must be willing to face your own cave moments.

The Cave Is Dark, But Necessary

Leadership can be glamorous in the stories we hear: accolades, promotions, success.

But real leadership? It's messy.

The cave is a place of:

- Isolation: Leadership can feel lonely. Decisions rest on your shoulders. You may feel misunderstood or unsupported.
- Failure: Mistakes happen. Plans fall apart. Sometimes you feel like you're the only one who sees the cracks.
- Fear: Fear of disappointing others, fear of not being enough, fear of the unknown.
- Reflection: The cave forces you to look inward, face your blind spots, and confront your weaknesses.

Yet, it's in this very darkness that growth ignites.

Why We Fear the Cave

Many leaders avoid "falling" or "failing" at all costs. We put on masks of confidence, polish, and control to hide the cracks.

But avoiding the cave leads to stagnation. Without challenge, you don't grow.

"Studies show that 60 percent of new managers underperform in their first two years, often due to a lack of support and training during early challenges." (Source: *CEB/Gartner*, 2016)

"Growth and comfort do not coexist."—*Ginni Rometty*

The fear of discomfort is natural, but it's a barrier to true leadership transformation.

What Falling Into the Cave Looks Like in Leadership

Your "cave moment" may take different shapes:

- A major project failure that threatens your credibility.
- A tough conversation that shakes your confidence.

- Receiving harsh feedback that challenges your self-perception.
- Feeling overwhelmed by competing demands and unclear priorities.
- Experiencing personal struggles health, family, or mental wellness that bleed into your work.
- Isolation at the top where you carry burdens alone.

Each is a kind of fall an entry into your cave.

The Cave as a Place of Transformation, Not Defeat

The cave is not a prison. It is a crucible.

Like steel forged by fire, leadership is refined by adversity.

Bruce Wayne emerges from the cave not defeated, but *reborn* equipped with clarity, purpose, and resolve. His trials become his strength.

The same is true for you.

When you lean into your cave moments, you develop:

- Resilience: The ability to bounce back from setbacks.
- Humility: Recognizing your limits and valuing others' strengths.
- Empathy: Understanding the struggles of those you lead because you've been there too.
- Authenticity: Showing up as your true self, flaws and all.

Batman's Allies: You Don't Have to Face the Cave Alone

Even Batman has allies: Alfred, Lucius Fox, and Commissioner Gordon.

No leader should go it alone.

Ask yourself:

- Who are my trusted advisers or mentors?
- Who can I confide in during difficult times?
- How can I build a support system within my team and beyond?

Support doesn't eliminate the cave but makes it navigable.

The Transformation: From Hero to Human Guide

How Servant Leaders Navigate the Cave Differently

For servant leaders, the cave journey is distinct because their leadership focus extends beyond themselves; it's deeply tied to the people they serve. This means they don't just wrestle with personal challenges but also carry the weight of others' struggles. Yet, this doesn't mean bearing it all alone or in silence. Instead, servant leaders lean into vulnerability, sharing their stories authentically and thoughtfully to build genuine connection and trust. They invite support, foster collaboration, and model a growth mindset that reframes failure and falling as natural, essential steps on the leadership path, not signs of weakness. "Research from *Harvard Business Review* found that leaders who display vulnerability in appropriate ways are 4.2 times more likely to be trusted by their employees." (Source: *Harvard Business Review Analytic Services*, 2019)

Finding Purpose in the Darkness

The cave isn't merely a dark trial to endure; it is a source of profound insight and renewed purpose. Like Bruce Wayne emerging from his ordeal with clarity and resolve, leaders who lean into their cave moments discover a deeper connection to their mission and a sharpened sense of why they lead. This transformation turns adversity into a guiding light, equipping leaders to empathize with others' struggles and to lead with both strength and compassion.

From Hero to Human Guide

Leadership stories often spotlight the hero; the one with all the answers, the fixer, the expert. But true leadership, especially servant leadership, is about evolving beyond that myth. Emerging from the cave signals a shift from striving for invincibility to embracing humanity. It means becoming a compassionate guide who walks alongside others in their hardest moments, rather than towering above them. Leaders who have faced and risen from their own struggles create psychological safety by normalizing growth, fear, failure, and vulnerability. They foster environments where authenticity thrives, and people feel safe to bring their whole selves to work. This transformation from hero to human guide builds deeper trust, resilience, and connection within teams and organizations.

Practical Steps to Lean Into Your Cave Moments

1. **Name Your Cave**
   Identify what you're facing honestly. Naming the struggle reduces its power.
2. **Allow Yourself to Feel**
   Don't rush past fear, frustration, or doubt. Sit with them long enough to understand what they're telling you.
3. **Reflect and Journal**
   Writing helps process emotions and clarifies thoughts. What lessons does this cave hold?
4. **Seek Perspective**
   Talk to mentors or peers who have faced similar challenges.
5. **Develop a Plan**
   What small steps can you take to move through the cave instead of being stuck in it?
6. **Share With Your Team**
   Vulnerability fosters trust and inspires others to bring their whole selves.

The Cave and the Light: Finding Purpose in Darkness

Your cave experience isn't just a trial it's a *transformational gift.*

It clarifies your purpose.

It deepens your connection to your mission.

It equips you to lead others through their own caves.

Batman's darkness is what makes him the hero Gotham needs.

Your leadership darkness can illuminate a path for your team.

Reflective Exercise: Your Cave Journey

Take 20–30 minutes in a quiet space with a journal or device.

1. **Identify Your Cave**
   - What is a current or past leadership challenge that felt like "falling into the cave?"
   - Describe it in detail. What emotions did you feel? Fear? Isolation? Frustration?
2. **Explore Your Response**
   - How did you respond in the moment?
   - Did you resist, retreat, lean in, or seek help?
   - What impact did your response have on you and your team?
3. **Extract the Lessons**
   - What did this cave moment teach you about yourself?
   - How did it change your perspective on leadership?
4. **Identify Allies and Support**
   - Who helped you through this moment or could help you now?
   - How can you build or strengthen your support network?
5. **Create Your Cave Action Plan**
   - What one or two steps can you take this week to lean into your current or future cave moments?
   - How will you show up differently?
6. **Write Your Cave Leadership Commitment**

   Finish this sentence:

   "I commit to facing my cave moments with courage and vulnerability because I know they will shape me into the leader my team needs."

   No one becomes Batman without falling into the cave. No leader rises without wrestling with darkness.

   Your cave is not a sign of weakness; it's the birthplace of strength.

   Embrace your cave moments. Let them forge resilience, empathy, and purpose.

   Because from the depths of the cave, your true leadership rises.

The Cave Teaches You to Lead in the Light—Not Hide From the Dark

But here's what's most overlooked about the cave:

It doesn't just shape who you become, it reshapes how you lead.

The cave isn't a personal hardship you overcome and then forget. It's a leadership classroom. A crucible that sharpens your ability to serve, see, and support others in their own struggles.

And the leaders who emerge the strongest?

They don't come back pretending the cave didn't happen.

They bring the **wisdom of that darkness** into the light and use it to guide others.

From Grit to Grace: What the Cave Builds That Performance Reviews Miss

There are strengths the cave gives you that no metric or feedback form can fully capture. These aren't skills, they're qualities. And they shape the core of servant leadership.

Here are just a few:

1. **Inner Stillness**
   When everything collapses and you survive; you no longer flinch at every crisis. You develop a calm center. You become the nonanxious presence that steadies others.
2. **Discernment**
   After falling hard, you stop sweating the superficial. You learn to tell the difference between urgent and important, noise and truth, ego and wisdom.
3. **Depth**
   You become more than a title or role. You become someone who leads with a full heart, not just a sharp mind. People can feel it—and follow it.

4. **Grace for Others**
   When you've failed, you stop punishing others for falling short. You create space for imperfection, learning, and comeback stories.

These aren't "soft" skills.

They're **essential leadership currencies** especially in today's culture of burnout, disconnection, and rapid change.

Real-Life Cave: From Crisis to Cultural Breakthrough

Take the story of Jacob, a hospital department leader who had always prided himself on excellence. He ran a tight ship, hit every metric, and rarely showed emotion.

Then his team missed a critical deadline, resulting in a cascade of stress and client complaints. He felt responsible, ashamed, and paralyzed. That was his cave.

But instead of doubling down on control, Jacob did something different:

- He called a teamwide meeting not to assign blame, but to admit his own missteps.
- He shared how the weight of perfectionism had driven him to overfunction and underlisten.
- He invited feedback, asked for help, and cocreated a new rhythm with his team.

What happened next?

Morale didn't plummet. It skyrocketed.

His team didn't see a weak leader; they saw a *human* one.

And from that cave moment, a new culture had been born;
one rooted in humility, flexibility, and shared ownership.

Jacob's fall became his turning point.

So can yours.

How to Lead *After* the Cave: Five Transformative Shifts

Once you've been through your cave and come out with clarity, you don't just return to your old patterns. You begin to lead differently. More grounded. More awake.

Here's what that shift looks like in practice:

1. **From Fixing to Listening**
   Instead of trying to solve everyone's problems immediately, you create space for them to process. You become a deep listener, not a chronic rescuer.
2. **From Projection to Presence**
   You stop leading based on how things *look* and start showing up for how things *are*. You stay present with discomfort instead of avoiding it.
3. **From Control to Trust**
   The cave taught you what happens when everything spins out. Now you know you can survive. So, you trust your team more freely and micromanage less.
4. **From Image to Integrity**
   You let go of appearances and lead with honesty. You're willing to say, "I don't know," or "I need help," and that builds deep trust.
5. **From Self-Protecting to People-Developing**
   The cave made you strong enough to hold space for others' caves. You invest in growth, not just outcomes.

Integrating the Cave Into Your Leadership Identity

The final evolution isn't just recovering from the cave; it's integrating it into who you are.

You stop hiding that part of your story.
You own it.
You lead with it not in a performative way, but as a grounding presence that says:

"You don't have to be perfect here. Just real. We'll grow through it together."

Your people won't follow you because you're always confident.
They'll follow you because you're always *true.*

So, when the cave calls, don't resist it.
Enter it with intention.
Learn what it came to teach you.
Then rise not just for yourself, but for those you're called to lead.

What the Cave Leaves Behind: The Leadership Scar That Strengthens

When someone survives a cave moment, they don't walk out the same way they walked in. The light may return, but the cave always leaves something behind a scar, a reminder, a shift. And though we often celebrate the "comeback," it's this internal shift that matters most.

Great leaders don't just rise they *carry.* They carry new values, new rhythms, and a refined sense of what matters the most. The cave doesn't just forge resilience; it reorients purpose.

So what does that look like on the other side?

You Start Choosing Substance Over Speed

After the cave, you no longer chase outcomes just to check a box. You slow down enough to *mean* what you do and invite others to do the same. Whether it's a staff meeting, a policy change, or a new hire, you're more intentional. You ask: *Will this build culture or just maintain appearances?*

You stop measuring success only by what's visible. You begin to lead from the invisible—the morale, the alignment, the trust.

You Begin to Redefine What "Strong Leadership" Looks Like

Before the cave, strength might have meant certainty, decisiveness, and control. After the cave? Strength looks like staying steady when others spiral. It looks like naming the elephant in the room. It looks like owning your part, even when it's uncomfortable.

And perhaps most importantly, it looks like *letting others see your scar without letting it define you.*

You don't share your cave story for sympathy; you share it to normalize humanity in leadership. You lead not just from what you know, but from *what you've lived.*

You Build Systems That Catch People *Before* They Fall

Once you've walked through darkness, you're far more attuned to the signs that others are approaching their own cave. You start to create structures of care: mental health check-ins, grace-filled reviews, peer mentoring, and time to reset.

You begin to lead proactively, not reactively.

You ask different questions:

- *How are you really?*
- *What feels heavy right now?*
- *Where do you need support before you break?*

That shift from pushing performance to cultivating resilience is the mark of someone who has done deep, inner work.

The Cave Creates Culture Shapers, Not Just Managers

Many leaders can manage a team. But leaders shaped by the cave don't just manage, they cultivate.

They don't push people toward goals alone, they pull them toward meaning.

They make space for real conversations.
They model boundaries.
They normalize recovery.

These leaders aren't performative. They're present.
They don't need to be the hero anymore.
They've become the guide.

And in today's world, that kind of leadership is rare and revolutionary.

Because no one becomes Batman without falling into the cave. But no one becomes the *leader their team truly needs* until they return carrying the light.

PART III

Evolving and Adapting

CHAPTER 9

Just Like a VHS—It's Time to Be Obsolete

In this chapter, we explore how outdated leadership styles; what we call "VHS leadership" —no longer serve today's fast-changing workplace. Just as VHS tapes gave way to streaming platforms, leaders must evolve beyond rigid, control-based habits to meet the needs of modern teams. Through practical examples, mindset shifts, and a call to unlearn legacy thinking, this chapter challenges readers to embrace adaptability, emotional intelligence, and servant leadership. It offers actionable steps and reflection exercises to help leaders move forward with courage and relevance in a constantly evolving world.

Remember VHS tapes?

Those bulky plastic rectangles once filled our living rooms and our lives with family movie nights, favorite shows recorded off TV, and home videos we watched over and over. Rewinding was a ritual. Tracking issues were normal. And for decades, VHS was how we experienced entertainment at home.

But then something better came along.

DVDs arrived: clearer, more compact, and faster. And not long after, streaming revolutionized the entire industry. Suddenly, we could access anything, anytime, anywhere with no clutter, no waiting, and no rewinding. VHS didn't disappear overnight. But it didn't take long before it felt … obsolete.

Leadership is going through the same evolution.

What once worked brilliantly—hierarchy, control, consistency—now feels clunky, inefficient, even harmful in today's workplace. The pace of change, the needs of the modern workforce, and the growing demand for purpose, inclusion, and empathy have shifted the leadership landscape.

Holding onto outdated styles is like insisting that your business still needs a VHS player in a streaming world.

It's time to let go.

Why Leaders Resist Evolving

Change is deeply uncomfortable not just practically, but psychologically. It threatens our comfort, disrupts our identity, and challenges the beliefs that got us here.

Most leaders don't resist evolving because they're stubborn. They resist because evolution feels risky, vulnerable, and uncertain.

Here are five common reasons leaders hold back:

- **Fear of losing control**—Traditional leadership often rewarded top-down decision making. Letting go of control can feel like losing authority.
- **Clinging to past success**—"This is how I got here" becomes a trap. What worked in the past becomes sacred even when it's no longer effective.
- **Routine feels safe**—Familiar patterns are comforting, even when they're no longer producing results.
- **Fear of failure**—Trying new methods invites critique, discomfort, and vulnerability. Many leaders would rather "stick to what they know."
- **Overwhelm**—When your plate is already full, the idea of "changing how you lead" feels like just one more impossible ask.

But here's the hard truth: *resisting change isn't neutral anymore.* It's harmful.

In today's workplace, stagnation doesn't just slow you down, it pushes your best people away. They feel it. They know when leadership is stuck in a format that doesn't fit their world. And they won't wait around for you to catch up.

The VHS Leader: What Obsolete Leadership Looks Like

We all know a VHS leader or have been one ourselves at some point. This isn't about judgment. It's about awareness.

Here are some signs you or someone in your organization might be leading like it's still 1995:

- Micromanaging instead of trusting.
- Communicating only in one direction, top-down.
- Resisting flexible work or new technology.
- Using outdated performance metrics.
- Repeating the same pep talks and wondering why they fall flat.
- Overlooking team well-being and culture.
- Focusing on appearances over actual impact.

Once upon a time, these behaviors symbolized control, strength, and decisiveness. Now they signal resistance, rigidity, and disconnect.

And the cost is high.

What Obsolete Leadership Actually Costs You

When leadership stays stuck, teams disengage. The damage doesn't always show up on a spreadsheet, but make no mistake, it's happening.

Here's how it shows up:

- **Engagement drops**—When people don't feel seen or heard, they check out.
- **Innovation stalls**—Fear replaces creativity. People stop challenging norms.
- **Top talent leaves**—The best employees want growth. They'll find it somewhere else if they can't find it with you.
- **Culture becomes stagnant**—Collaboration, enthusiasm, and inclusion fade.
- **Clients feel the drag**—An outdated team can't meet modern needs, and your customers notice.

Gallup research shows that managers account for at least 70 percent of the variance in employee engagement. Yet only one in three employees in the United States strongly agree that they are engaged at work. Leaders who cling to outdated, control-based styles are directly linked to disengagement, which Gallup estimates costs organizations $7.8 trillion annually in lost productivity worldwide. Obsolete leadership creates a culture of quiet quitting, low trust, and missed opportunities. It's not just a people problem. It's a business risk.

Streaming-Era Leadership: What Modern Leadership Looks Like

So, what does modern, "streaming-era" leadership look like?

It looks like adaptability. Like curiosity. Like trust.

Modern leaders don't cling to control. They build cultures that trust, include, and grow people. They don't just manage, they serve. A 2022 *McKinsey* study found that employees are five times more likely to stay at a company when they feel that their leaders are empathetic, supportive, and growth oriented. Conversely, workplaces with rigid, outdated leadership experience significantly higher turnover, especially among younger generations; 67 percent of Gen Z say they would leave a job if leadership lacked empathy.

Here's what that looks like in action:

- Empowering teams with autonomy, not just accountability.
- Building two-way communication, not broadcasting top-down messages.
- Embracing technology and digital tools that increase flexibility and efficiency.
- Encouraging continuous learning and development for everyone, including themselves.
- Modeling emotional intelligence, vulnerability, and empathy.
- Creating psychologically safe environments where people can be honest, bold, and creative.
- Encouraging shared ownership and purpose, not just performance.

This isn't a trendy leadership style. It's a survival strategy for thriving teams.

The Gift of Obsolescence

"Obsolete" doesn't sound like a gift but in leadership, it can be.

Intentional obsolescence means you're willing to name and release the leadership practices, behaviors, and beliefs that no longer serve your team or your mission.

It takes:

- **Humility** to admit what no longer works.
- **Clarity** to see the gap between intention and impact.
- **Courage** to change even if you're successful "as is."

It's not about abandoning your values. It's about honoring them better through new methods.

Legacy Thinking Can't Lead the Future

We all carry a bit of "legacy code" in our leadership DNA—things we picked up from past—managers, early jobs, or cultural expectations. Some of it is helpful. Some of it holds us back.

Legacy thinking often shows up in phrases like:

- "Back in my day…"
- "This generation just doesn't want to work."
- "If there's a problem, they'll come to me."

These aren't harmless statements. They're warning sign, reminders that our leadership lens may be outdated.

They don't help us lead this generation. Or the next.

Unlearning: The Secret to Lasting Leadership

Unlearning is one of the most underrated leadership skills of the 21st century.

It doesn't mean forgetting everything. It means loosening your grip on certainty.

It means asking:

Does this still serve the people I lead?

Unlearning looks like:

- Trading control for trust.
- Replacing "my way" with "our way."
- Swapping toughness for empathy.
- Choosing listening over lecturing.

It's the kind of leadership your team will *feel* and remember.

The Ego Is the Last Obsolete Format

Let's be real. The hardest part of evolution isn't strategy. It's ego.

Ego is the last thing most leaders are willing to let go of. It tells us:

- "I need to be the expert."
- "I'm responsible for having the answers."
- "I earned this authority I shouldn't have to change."

But ego is the enemy of servant leadership. It puts *you* at the center, when real leadership puts *others* there.

True leadership says:

"My job isn't to be the hero, it's to build heroes."

That's the difference between a legacy leader and a lasting one.

Five Practical Ways to Evolve Your Leadership

Want to start your evolution? Begin here:

1. **Audit Your Habits**
   List your current leadership approaches. What's still working? What feels outdated?

2. **Ask for Feedback**
   Don't assume. Ask your team: "Where could I grow?" "What do you need from me?"
3. **Invest in Learning**
   Stay curious; read, listen, attend, and engage with fresh ideas and perspectives.
4. **Experiment Often**
   Try one new behavior, format, or decision-making model. Reflect. Adjust. Repeat.
5. **Celebrate Change**
   Acknowledge your growth and the team's. Celebrate progress over perfection.

Reflective Exercise: Are You Leading Like a VHS Tape?

Take 30 minutes in a quiet space and answer:

1. What leadership habits am I holding onto that feel outdated?
2. Where have I seen signs my style isn't landing with my team?
3. What am I afraid of losing if I change how I lead?
4. What does modern, adaptive leadership look like for me?
5. What is one outdated practice I'll release and one new one I'll try this month?

Write this down:

"I commit to evolving my leadership by letting go of what no longer serves and embracing what truly empowers my team."

Final Thoughts: Let Go to Lead Forward

You don't need to abandon who you are as a leader. But you do need to evolve how you lead.

The world has moved beyond VHS tapes.

Your team has moved beyond legacy mindsets.

The moment you choose to grow, you're already doing what real leadership demands serving your people, staying relevant, and showing up fully human.

So let go. Lean in. Lead forward.

Because the best of your leadership isn't behind you. It's ahead.

CHAPTER 10

Trust Me, I'm a High Performer—Not a Pressure Cooker!

High performers are the driving force behind many successful teams, but too often they're treated like machines rather than people. This chapter explores the hidden costs of placing relentless pressure on top performers and introduces a servant leadership approach rooted in trust, autonomy, and well-being. You'll learn how to identify signs of burnout, shift from micromanagement to empowerment, and build a leadership culture where high performers don't just survive, they thrive. Through practical strategies, case studies, and reflection prompts, this chapter equips you to lead with empathy and create sustainable excellence through trust.

Introduction: The High Performer Dilemma

In almost every organization, high performers are the shining stars. They consistently deliver excellent results, take initiative, and inspire others with their work ethic. Naturally, leaders lean on these individuals to keep the gears turning and the mission advancing.

But there's a subtle, dangerous trap in how we often treat these top performers. We expect them to be unshakable, indefatigable engines of productivity; putting them under relentless pressure, pushing them to do more, faster, and better, all the time. We treat them like pressure cookers: sealed tightly, cranked up to max, expected to produce without pause.

This approach is not just unsustainable, it is harmful.

As a servant leader, your challenge is to trust your high performers, not pressure them. You must create an environment where their best work emerges from support and respect, not fear and exhaustion.

What It Means to Be a High Performer

High performers bring unique value to a team:

- Consistent excellence: They deliver quality work reliably, often ahead of deadlines.
- Ownership: They take responsibility and initiative without needing micromanagement.
- Problem-solving: They proactively address challenges and find innovative solutions.
- Inspiration: Their passion and dedication motivate peers to elevate their own work.
- Adaptability: They respond to changing circumstances with resilience and flexibility.

Yet, none of these qualities mean they are invincible or impervious to stress.

The Pressure Cooker Mentality: Why It's Toxic

Pressure cooker leadership is an all-too-common response to high performance:

- Unrealistic expectations: Assuming that because someone excels, they can always do more.
- Micromanagement under guise of oversight: Increasing scrutiny because "high stakes" demand it.
- Ignoring warning signs: Dismissing signs of fatigue, stress, or disengagement as "just part of the job."
- Punishing failure: Viewing mistakes harshly instead of as opportunities to learn.
- One-size-fits-all demands: Expecting high performers to sacrifice work–life balance constantly.

Over time, this environment creates a pressure cooker effect where tension builds, and if not released, leads to burnout, mistakes, and eventual breakdown.

The True Cost of the Pressure Cooker: Beyond Burnout

Burnout is the most visible consequence, but the cost runs deeper:

- Declining creativity: Fear of mistakes shuts down innovation and risk-taking.
- Reduced loyalty: High performers feel undervalued and expendable, weakening retention.
- Toxic ripple effect: Stress and disengagement spread to other team members, lowering morale.
- Missed potential: Overworked individuals cannot perform at their peak or develop further.
- Damaged relationships: Trust between leader and team erodes, making collaboration difficult.

Burnout is estimated to cost US businesses up to $190 billion annually in health care expenses and productivity loss. High performers, due to consistently heavy workloads, are among the most vulnerable groups. This cost is too high for any leader or organization to ignore.

Building Trust: The Foundation of Sustainable High Performance

Trust transforms how high performers engage with their work:

- Trust that their leader has their back: Knowing mistakes won't lead to punishment but coaching.
- Trust in autonomy: Having freedom to innovate and make decisions within their role.
- Trust in open communication: Feeling safe to share struggles or ask for help without judgment.
- Trust in balance: Confidence that their well-being is valued as much as their output.

Gallup found that employees who strongly agree that their manager cares about their well-being are 69 percent less likely to actively search for a new job. For high performers, this highlights how trust and care directly drive retention. When trust is present, pressure becomes purposeful challenge energizing rather than draining.

Servant Leadership: The Antidote to Pressure Cooker Culture

Servant leaders put the needs of their people first. When working with high performers, this means:

- Listening deeply: Understanding individual motivations, stresses, and aspirations.
- Removing obstacles: Clearing away bureaucracy, unnecessary tasks, or distractions.
- Encouraging rest: Advocating for breaks, boundaries, and mental health practices.
- Acknowledging effort: Celebrating growth, process, and resilience, not just outcomes.
- Fostering psychological safety: Creating an environment where vulnerability is respected.
- Modeling humility: Admitting your own limits and being open to feedback.

This creates a culture where high performers feel genuinely supported, not just utilized.

But creating that culture isn't always simple. It requires leaders to intentionally build trust in ways that balance freedom with accountability, empowering high performers without losing sight of the mission. Let's explore what that trust equation looks like in practice.

The Trust Equation: How Leaders Create Freedom Without Losing Focus

In the fast-paced environments where high performers thrive, the line between trust and control is often blurry. Leaders want to give autonomy but fear losing grip on results. High performers crave freedom but worry about the cost of mistakes. The challenge? Building a trust equation that balances accountability with empowerment without tipping into micromanagement or neglect.

Trust isn't a blind leap. It's a dynamic, ongoing process that requires intention, clarity, and courage from both leaders and high performers. Here's how servant leaders get this right:

1. **Clarity Builds Confidence**

   Autonomy doesn't mean absence of guidance. On the contrary, clear expectations create a foundation for trust. When high performers know *exactly* what success looks like not just in terms of deliverables but also in behaviors, timelines, and communication norms; they can operate freely within those guardrails.

   Example:

   Imagine a high-performing project lead who knows her goal is to launch a new product feature by quarter-end. If she also understands that weekly check-ins are for alignment, not scrutiny, she can plan her work and pivot quickly without constant oversight.

   As a servant leader, your role is to cocreate this clarity:

   - Define outcomes, not just outputs.
   - Agree on decision-making boundaries.
   - Set standards for quality and communication.

   This removes ambiguity and creates psychological safety because the high performer isn't guessing what the leader wants or fearing arbitrary judgment.

2. **Trust Is Built on Small Bets and Feedback Loops**

   Trust grows incrementally, like a muscle exercised through small "bets" or opportunities to prove reliability. Rather than handing over huge responsibilities without support, servant leaders provide staged autonomy paired with constructive feedback.

   Try this approach:

   - Assign a manageable project piece and let the high performer run with it.
   - Observe, then provide specific feedback on what worked and what could improve.
   - Increase scope gradually as confidence grows.

Frequent, honest feedback; not just performance reviews is the currency of trust. It tells high performers they're valued and their development matters more than perfection.

3. **Empowerment Requires Letting Go**

   One of the hardest things for leaders is to relinquish control over how things get done. High performers often have their own ways of working that maximize efficiency and creativity. Micromanaging these details stifles their initiative and damages trust.

   Instead, servant leaders:

   - Focus on the *why* and *what,* leaving the *how* to the high performer.
   - Resist the urge to "fix" processes or redo work unless absolutely necessary.
   - Embrace the occasional mistake as a sign of growth and learning.

   This doesn't mean ignoring accountability; it means partnering in a way that respects autonomy.

4. **Prioritize Well-Being as a Leadership Metric**

   Sustainable high performance isn't just about outputs it's about energy, engagement, and resilience. Servant leaders recognize that pressure cooker culture slowly drains these vital resources.

   A key part of the trust equation is making well-being a visible priority:

   - Normalize conversations about mental health and burnout.
   - Encourage regular breaks and disconnecting after work hours.
   - Model vulnerability by sharing your own challenges and coping strategies.

   When leaders show they care about people as whole humans, high performers feel safer to bring their full selves to work and that fuels lasting excellence.

5. **Foster Peer Trust and Shared Responsibility**

   Trust isn't only vertical from leader to individual; it's also horizontal among team members. High performers flourish in environments where peer relationships are strong, collaborative, and supportive.

As a servant leader, you can:

- Facilitate team rituals that build connection (stand-ups, peer recognition, shared problem-solving).
- Encourage knowledge sharing and mentorship among high performers and others.
- Address toxic competitiveness or gatekeeping behaviors early.

A culture where peers trust each other creates a safety net, reducing isolation and distributing pressure more evenly.

6. **Leaders Must Own Their Impact on Trust**

Finally, building trust means examining your own behaviors and biases. Are you consistent in your words and actions? Do you show up authentically, admitting mistakes and asking for input? Do you reward trustworthiness and integrity as much as results?

Servant leaders are self-reflective and humble, recognizing that trust is fragile and must be actively nurtured every day.

The Trust Equation in Action: A Story From the Field

Trust = Clarity + Autonomy + Feedback + Support

Take the example of Casey, a senior technician at a growing hospital. Casey was a clear high performer but often frustrated by his manager's tendency to micromanage timelines and task lists. Feeling stifled, Casey started withdrawing, and his creativity stalled.

Recognizing the risk, the manager adopted a servant leadership mindset:

- She sat down with Casey to clarify expectations and understand his working style.
- They agreed on broad milestones but left Casey free to design his own workflow.
- The manager scheduled weekly "growth chats" focused on Casey's development, not just deliverables.
- She openly acknowledged when she struggled to let go of control and asked Casey for feedback on her leadership.

Over months, Casey's engagement soared. He started volunteering to lead new initiatives and mentoring newer staff members. Trust had turned pressure into partnership.

Practical Steps to Start Balancing Trust and Autonomy Today

- **Cocreate clear goals:** Use collaborative goal-setting sessions.
- **Establish regular, low-stakes check-ins:** Build feedback into everyday rhythms.
- **Challenge yourself to pause before intervening:** Ask, "Is this a teachable moment or a control moment?"
- **Celebrate learning, not just winning:** Frame mistakes as part of growth.
- **Encourage your team to set boundaries:** Normalize saying no and resting.
- **Invest in team bonding:** Build peer trust deliberately.
- **Model vulnerability:** Share your leadership journey authentically.

Reflective Prompt

Ask yourself:

- When was the last time I trusted a high performer to do something their way?
- How do I respond when things don't go perfectly?
- What small step can I take this week to lean more into trust and less into control?

Remember: Trust is not a one-time gift. It's an ongoing leadership practice that, when done well, transforms high performers from pressure cookers into empowered partners; driving your organization forward with sustainable excellence.

Knowing how to build and maintain this trust is critical because when it breaks down, high performers start to show signs of strain. Recognizing those early warning signals allows servant leaders to intervene thoughtfully, before pressure becomes a breaking point.

Signs Your High Performers Are Feeling Like Pressure Cookers

Beware of these red flags:

- Increased absenteeism or tardiness.
- Decreased quality of work or missed deadlines.
- Withdrawal from team interactions.
- Expressing frustration or cynicism openly or subtly.
- Decline in enthusiasm or motivation.
- Physical or emotional exhaustion.

If you see these signs, it's time to reassess your leadership approach and rebuild trust.

Case Study: Turning Pressure Into Partnership

Consider Emily, a veterinary technician who was known for taking on complex cases and working long hours. Her manager, initially proud of her dedication, began assigning more responsibilities without checking in.

Eventually, Emily's performance slipped, and she stopped volunteering for difficult cases. A candid conversation revealed that she was overwhelmed and felt no support.

The manager shifted to a servant leadership approach:

- Scheduled regular one-on-one check-ins focusing on Emily's well-being.
- Redistributed workload fairly among the team.
- Encouraged Emily to set boundaries and take days off without guilt.
- Publicly recognized Emily's efforts and encouraged peer support.

Emily's engagement rebounded, and she became even more effective; now working smarter, not harder.

Strategies to Build Trust With High Performers

1. **Set Clear, Realistic Expectations**
   Make sure that high performers know what success looks like, including boundaries around work hours and rest.
2. **Prioritize Open Dialogue**
   Create safe spaces for honest conversations about stress, workload, and needs.
3. **Delegate With Autonomy**
   Trust high performers to manage their projects and decisions; offer guidance, not control.
4. **Normalize Taking Breaks**
   Model and encourage rest, showing that recovery is part of high performance.
5. **Provide Growth Opportunities**
   Align challenging assignments with career goals, avoiding busywork that drains energy.
6. **Recognize Holistic Success**
   Celebrate process improvements, teamwork, learning, and resilience alongside results.

Reflective Exercise: Building Trust, Not Pressure

Set aside 30 minutes for this deep reflection:

1. **Evaluate Your Approach:**
   - How do I currently treat my high performers?
   - Do they feel supported or pressured? Give examples.
2. **Identify Pressure Points:**
   - Are there signs any high performers are burning out or disengaging?
   - How have I responded to these signs?

3. **Explore Trust-Building Opportunities:**
   - How often do I check in on well-being, not just results?
   - What changes can I make to foster autonomy and open communication?
4. **Commit to Change:**
   - What's one specific action I will take this week to shift from pressure to trust?
   - How will I communicate this commitment to my team?
5. **Affirm Your Leadership Philosophy:**
   Complete the sentence:

   "I commit to leading my high performers with empathy, respect, and trust because sustainable excellence depends on people, not pressure."

   This isn't just theory; it's your next leadership move. Don't just reflect. Act. Because your high performers need more than recognition. They need you.

Final Thoughts: From Pressure Cooker to Trusted Partner

High performers are your greatest assets, but they are not machines.

Treating them like pressure cookers is a fast track to burnout, disengagement, and loss.

Instead, lead them as trusted partners; listen, support, and empower. Build a culture where trust fuels performance, creativity, and loyalty.

When you do, your high performers won't just survive; they'll thrive, and so will your entire organization.

CHAPTER 11

Like *The Breakfast Club*, Leadership Is About Everyone Belonging

Belonging isn't a soft skill, it's the foundation of trust, innovation, and retention. In this chapter, you'll learn why fostering a culture of belonging is essential for today's teams, how servant leaders build it, and what practical steps you can take to ensure that every team member feels safe, seen, and significant.

When *The Breakfast Club* premiered in 1985, it was instantly iconic not just because of its soundtrack or its one-liners, but because of how deeply it captured something most of us never outgrow: the desire to belong.

Five teenagers, each from a different clique; the brain, the athlete, the basket case, the princess, and the criminal sit in a library for Saturday detention. They start the day as strangers (or worse, stereotypes) but leave having seen one another fully for the first time. Not just the labels, but the fears, pain, dreams, and truth behind them.

At its core, *The Breakfast Club* is about breaking down barriers, seeing past assumptions, and understanding that we all want to be known and accepted for who we really are.

This isn't just a coming-of-age concept. It's a leadership imperative.

Because in business, as in that library on a Saturday, real transformation happens when people feel they truly belong.

Why Belonging Is the Leadership Superpower You're Overlooking

We've all been taught to focus on performance. On productivity. On goals and key performance indicators (KPIs) and benchmarks.

But here's the thing: none of those matter if people don't feel safe, connected, and valued.

Research from *Harvard Business Review* and Deloitte confirms that belonging is a major driver of engagement, innovation, and retention. When people feel excluded even subtly they hold back. They disconnect. They leave.

But when people feel like they *matter*, they:

- Speak up with new ideas.
- Collaborate more effectively.
- Take healthy risks.
- Invest more of their energy and heart into their work.
- Stay.

A team that belongs together performs together.

The Modern Workplace Has a Belonging Crisis

Even in the most well-intentioned businesses, many people feel unseen or "othered":

- The technician who feels ignored by the medical team.
- The introvert who's labeled as "aloof" instead of respected for their quiet insight.
- The older team member who's dismissed as "stuck in their ways."
- The receptionist who never gets invited to decision-making conversations.
- The BIPOC team member who's tired of being the only person of color in leadership meetings.
- The new employee who still feels like they're intruding on a "family."

Research by BetterUp shows that workplace exclusion creates feelings of anxiety and disengagement, leading to a 40 percent decrease in team collaboration and significantly higher stress levels.

No one wants to feel like a guest in a house they work hard to build.

Leadership is about tearing down the walls the cliques, silos, and subtle power dynamics and replacing them with a culture where every voice matters, and every person feels seen.

How Belonging Gets Built: What Servant Leaders Do Differently

Servant leadership flips the script from "What can I get out of you?" to "How can I help you thrive?" And that's the perfect foundation for belonging.

Here's how servant leaders build it:

1. **They Break the Labels**
   Just like *The Breakfast Club* showed us, people are more than the job titles or first impressions we slap on them. Servant leaders dig deeper.
   Try this: Invite someone you don't normally connect with to share something meaningful about their journey. You might be shocked at what you learn and how your perspective changes.
2. **They Make Inclusion Intentional**
   Belonging doesn't just "happen." It requires deliberate action, systems, and feedback loops that tell people: "You're not just allowed to be here you're wanted here."
   A *Harvard Business Review* study found that employees who feel a strong sense of belonging show a 56 percent increase in job performance, a 50 percent drop in turnover risk, and a 75 percent reduction in sick days. Try this: Rotate meeting leads. Invite new voices into strategic discussions. Say "What do you think?" more often.
3. **They Model Vulnerability**
   When leaders drop the mask, others feel safe to do the same. Vulnerability is the fastest path to belonging.
   Try this: Share your own past missteps, fears, or lessons during team huddles. It humanizes you and gives others permission to do the same.
4. **They Celebrate Individuality Without Tokenizing**
   Real belonging means you don't have to shrink or perform to fit in. Servant leaders create cultures where difference is celebrated, not smoothed out.

Try this: Spotlight team member stories in newsletters or meetings. Acknowledge unique skills, backgrounds, and passions.

5. **They Address the "Invisible Work"**

   Often, the people doing the emotional labor of keeping culture kind, onboarding new hires, or smoothing conflict aren't formally recognized. That hurts belonging.

   Try this: Publicly thank the "glue people." Offer recognition and responsibility, not just applause.

Belonging in Action: Culture, Safety, and Shared Responsibility

Belonging isn't just about being included on paper, it's about feeling safe, valued, and connected in daily work life. That kind of culture doesn't build itself. It takes conscious action from leaders and teams.

At the heart of this work is psychological safety, the quiet engine that powers belonging. Coined by Harvard professor Amy Edmondson, psychological safety describes a team environment where people trust one another, feel respected, and are comfortable being themselves, especially when it's uncomfortable.

When psychological safety is present:

- People ask questions without fear of looking foolish.
- They challenge ideas respectfully.
- They admit mistakes and learn from them.
- They take creative risks and offer bold ideas.

This matters because belonging requires vulnerability. You can't feel like you belong if you're constantly self-editing or guarding your identity. It's not just about being invited into the room, it's about feeling free to speak, contribute, and be your whole self once you're there.

Just like in *The Breakfast Club*, real connection happens when people dare to show up authentically. Their moment of transformation came when they stopped performing and started sharing the fears, hopes, and truths that made them human. As leaders, we must create the kind of culture where that kind of vulnerability isn't just allowed, it's welcomed.

But belonging isn't the leader's job alone. It's a shared responsibility, and teams have a crucial role to play.

Team members build belonging when they:

- Call out exclusionary behaviors, even the subtle ones.
- Welcome newcomers with curiosity instead of critique.
- Recognize diverse work styles and communication preferences.
- Celebrate each other's wins and stories, not just achievements.
- Stay mindful of microinequities small slights that can erode trust over time.

When a team actively chooses to care, listen, and support not just work side-by-side, their belonging grows naturally.

Belonging in action is about *culture*, *safety*, and *shared responsibility.* It's not a one-time initiative, it's an everyday practice of noticing, honoring, and uplifting humanity in each other.

The Intersection of Belonging and Equity: Moving Beyond "Fit"

Sometimes, leaders confuse belonging with "cultural fit," a notion that can unintentionally exclude diverse voices. Belonging means feeling accepted without having to change who you are to "fit in."

This subtle but crucial distinction is at the heart of equitable leadership. It means:

- **Valuing diverse perspectives as a source of strength**, not as a problem to manage.
- **Reexamining hiring and promotion practices to remove bias** and ensure that opportunities are genuinely open.
- **Challenging norms that privilege certain personalities or communication styles** over others.
- **Celebrating differences as an asset rather than a barrier**.

When belonging is defined by acceptance rather than conformity, teams become more creative, resilient, and sustainable.

Technology and Belonging: Digital Spaces Can Bridge or Break Connection

In today's hybrid and remote workplaces, belonging faces new challenges and opportunities.

Digital communication can sometimes feel transactional and disconnected. Without the cues of body language or casual hallway chats, people can feel isolated or invisible.

But technology can also be a powerful tool for belonging when used thoughtfully:

- **Virtual "watercooler" channels** that encourage informal connection.
- **Video check-ins that allow for face-to-face interaction** even across distance.
- **Collaborative platforms that democratize input and spotlight contributions**.
- **Asynchronous communication that respects different time zones and work rhythms**.

Servant leaders need to be intentional about how they design digital interactions to foster belonging, not just efficiency.

Belonging as a Catalyst for Resilience and Innovation

Belonging isn't just a feel-good bonus. It's a strategic advantage.

Teams where people feel they belong are more resilient in the face of setbacks. They rebound faster because trust and psychological safety allow them to tackle problems openly.

They innovate more because belonging encourages risk-taking, experimentation, and the free exchange of ideas without fear.

In times of rapid change or crisis like a pandemic or organizational restructuring, the power of belonging can determine whether a team fractures or pulls together.

Real-Life Example: From Silos to Solidarity at a Veterinary Practice

In a busy animal hospital, a divide had formed: doctors upstairs, techs in the treatment area, and CSRs at the front desk. Communication was transactional. Tensions were high. People worked around each other, not *with* each other.

Then, the leadership team did something radical: they implemented a "Belonging Reset."

- They held small, cross-functional lunches focused on storytelling and "why I do this work."
- They set up a shared Slack channel where every team member could give "micro shout-outs" to one another.
- They launched a rotating "Day in the Life" series, where one person a week shared their role and struggles with the full team.

The result?

More empathy. Better communication. Deeper trust. A genuine sense that everyone was rowing the boat in the same direction.

Performance didn't dip. It skyrocketed.

Practical Ways to Build Belonging Every Day

- Greet people by name, every single day.
- Use inclusive language ("we" instead of "you guys," "team" instead of "staff").
- Ask questions that invite perspective: "What's something you wish others knew about your role?"
- Have culture touchpoints, not just operational ones (e.g., gratitude circles, check-in rounds, story shares).
- Remove physical and conversational barriers (don't let "the back" and "the front" become rival territories).
- Put belonging in your metrics: Pulse surveys, feedback loops, even part of your leadership performance reviews.

Reflective Exercise: Your Belonging Audit

Take 30–40 minutes in a quiet space. Be honest. This exercise isn't about guilt, it's about growth.

1. **Look Around Your Team**
   - Who speaks most in meetings? Who stays silent?
   - Who gets invited into strategic conversations?
   - Who hasn't gotten feedback in a while?
   - Who might feel like an outsider?
2. **Examine Yourself**
   - When did I last assume something about a team member that might have been wrong?
   - Do I give everyone the same energy, or just those I "click" with?
   - Do I make room for difference, or do I subtly reward sameness?
3. **Take Ownership**
   Complete this sentence:

   "The biggest way I unintentionally limit belonging in my team is …"

   Now complete this one:

   "The smallest, most powerful thing I can do this week to foster more belonging is …"
4. **Make Belonging a Leadership Value**
   Commit to embedding belonging into your leadership:

   Write your personal leadership commitment statement:

   "As a servant leader, I will lead a team where every person feels safe, seen, and significant. I will break labels, celebrate difference, and build a culture where everyone belongs not just because it feels good, but because it makes us stronger."

Final Scene: Leadership That Unites

At the end of *The Breakfast Club*, the students walk out of detention changed. Not because someone gave them a better GPA or a promotion but because, for the first time, they felt understood.

That's what true leadership does.

It doesn't just assign tasks or track results. It cultivates connection. It makes people feel like they're part of something greater. It tells them, "You don't need to be anyone else to belong here."

As a servant leader, your greatest power is not in how much you know or how fast you move. It's in how deeply you care and how boldly you build belonging.

So go ahead. Break the labels. Invite the quiet voices. Celebrate the rebels, the athletes, the artists, the caregivers, the introverts, the new hires, the veterans.

Make your leadership a space where everyone can walk in and say:

"This is where I belong."

CHAPTER 12

Great Leaders Are Communication Chameleons

Great leadership isn't just about what you say, it's about how your message is received. In this chapter, we explore how adaptable communication like a chameleon adjusting to its surroundings is essential for servant leadership. You'll learn how to recognize different communication styles on your team, avoid common breakdowns, and build trust through empathy, clarity, and presence. By expanding your communication range and tuning into your audience, you create deeper connection, stronger collaboration, and more effective leadership.

In the animal kingdom, chameleons are known for one thing: adaptability. They shift their color not to deceive, but to respond to their environment. It's protection, connection, and survival.

Great leaders do the same with communication.

They don't just talk. They tune in. They shift tone, format, pace, and even platform based on who they're speaking to. They know how to read the room, the person, and the moment, and adjust accordingly to ensure that their message is received as intended.

This isn't inauthentic. It's intentional. It's not manipulation, it's empathy in motion. Leadership requires communication fluency, and servant leadership demands it at a higher level. If we want to serve, guide, and inspire, we must be willing to speak the language of those we lead.

What Happens When You Don't Adapt

Let's get real. You can have the best idea in the world, the clearest vision, or the most heartfelt feedback, but if the way you deliver it doesn't connect with the person you're speaking to, it falls flat.

Misalignment leads to:

- Confusion ("I thought they understood what I meant").
- Frustration ("They never listen").
- Resentment ("I'm always the last to know").
- Disengagement ("This doesn't feel like it's for me").

Research by the Economist Intelligence Unit reported that poor workplace communication leads to $62.4 million in lost productivity annually per company (average, for firms with 100,000 employees).

Often, these aren't skill issues, they're communication breakdowns.

Communication isn't about what you said. It's about what they heard, understood, and absorbed.

Communication Versus Connection

Here's the real secret: communication isn't about transmission, it's about transformation.

- Did your words change how someone feels or sees something?
- Did they spark action or clarity?
- Did they affirm a person's value or direction?

That's the goal. That's the magic of chameleon communication. It's not about being slick, it's about being of service.

Common Communication Styles on Your Team

Every team is a mixed bag. And that's a good thing if you know how to navigate it.

The Analyst

- Needs: Logic, structure, and data.
- Communication Tip: Get to the point with evidence. Avoid ambiguity.

The Empath

- Needs: Emotional safety and tone awareness.
- Communication Tip: Lead with care. Acknowledge feelings before facts.

The Activator

- Needs: Action, clarity, and brevity.
- Communication Tip: Be concise. Give the next steps. Avoid overexplaining.

The Collaborator

- Needs: Dialogue and consensus.
- Communication Tip: Invite opinions. Emphasize shared goals.

The Visionary

- Needs: Purpose and inspiration.
- Communication Tip: Connect to big picture. Use stories or metaphors.

Style	Needs	Tips
Analyst	Logic, structure, data	Use evidence; avoid ambiguity
Empath	Emotional safety, tone	Lead with care; acknowledge feelings
Activator	Action, clarity, brevity	Be concise; give clear next steps
Collaborator	Dialogue, consensus	Invite opinions; emphasize shared outcomes
Visionary	Purpose, inspiration	Use big-picture language; share stories

Knowing who you're talking to and adjusting accordingly makes you more effective, approachable, and trustworthy.

Story From the Field: Communication Cure at the Clinic

In a veterinary clinic I consulted with, the lead DVM Doctor of Veterinary Medicine was known for giving fast, direct updates during rounds. Short. Efficient. Bullet-pointed.

To her, it was respectful: quick and clear.

To her team? It felt cold and dismissive.

Morale was tanking. Misunderstandings were common. People were afraid to ask questions.

With coaching, she changed her approach:

- During huddles, she began opening with one to two minutes of gratitude.
- She checked in individually with team members after meetings.
- She used analogies and stories to explain complex cases.

Within weeks, the mood shifted. Her message hadn't changed; her delivery had. And that made all the difference.

Building Your Adaptable Communication Practice

Becoming a communication chameleon isn't about being scripted or inauthentic, it's about being present, intentional, and focused on connection. Great servant leaders don't just speak well; they adjust how they communicate based on the needs of their audience. They read the moment, the individual, and the context, then tailor their delivery so their message is not just said but received.

Adaptability in communication is not an innate talent. It is a skill, a discipline, and a practice developed over time through observation, feedback, and reflection.

1. **Start With Listening**

   Effective communication begins with listening, not speaking. Before delivering a message, pause to assess:
   - What is the tone in the room?
   - What kind of energy is the other person bringing?
   - What might they need right now; clarity, empathy, motivation, reassurance?

   Servant leaders treat listening as a form of service. The intent is not just to respond but to understand and honor the other person's experience. A study in the *International Journal of Listening* found that leaders rated high in active listening were perceived as 40 percent more effective and had stronger team trust and collaboration outcomes.

One powerful habit is to follow up any message with a simple clarification prompt, such as:

"Here's what I meant, how did that land for you?"

This allows space for alignment and mutual clarity.

2. **Mirror With Respect**

   People feel more open and comfortable when they sense that you're meeting them where they are. Mirroring someone's communication style gently and respectfully can create a stronger sense of connection and trust.

   If someone is fast-paced and energetic, respond with focused brevity. If they're quiet and reflective, slow down. If they seem overwhelmed, lead with calm empathy rather than urgency. This isn't mimicry, it's emotional alignment.

   Adaptation builds trust when it's grounded in sincerity.

3. **Layer Your Communication**

   Different people process information in different ways. Strong communicators use multiple methods to reinforce a message.

   Say it clearly in a meeting. Follow up in writing. Use a relevant story or metaphor. Include visual aids if helpful. Then ask for confirmation or questions. Repetition isn't redundancy, it's reinforcement. The more channels you use, the more likely your message is to stick.

4. **Expand Your Range Through Intentional Practice**

   One way to build adaptability is to experiment, especially in lower-stakes settings. If you typically offer detailed explanations, practice summarizing. If you tend to be very direct, try softening your tone or asking more questions. If you usually default to e-mail, pick up the phone or walk over to someone's desk.

   Pay attention to the response. Was the message received more clearly? Did the tone foster openness or defensiveness? Use these moments as data points in refining your style.

   This process isn't about becoming someone you're not. It's about expanding your range and learning to lead across differences.

5. **Invite Feedback and Be Willing to Adjust**

   Adaptability depends on self-awareness and that's best developed through feedback. Ask your team how your communication is landing. Encourage them to share when a message wasn't clear or when your tone missed the mark.

Model humility in the process by saying:

"I want to make sure I communicated that clearly. Did it come across the way I intended?"

At the same time, take note of nonverbal cues or patterns. If people frequently ask for clarification, seem confused, or disengage, those are signs to reflect on your delivery—not just your content.

6. **Respect Cultural and Contextual Differences**

   In diverse teams, communication styles and preferences often vary. What feels energizing to one person may feel overwhelming to another. What sounds respectful to one team member may feel abrupt to someone else.

   Leaders must learn to adjust across cultures, personalities, and professional backgrounds. This includes understanding whether directness or subtlety is preferred, whether decisions are typically made collectively or individually, and how feedback is best delivered.

   Awareness of these nuances fosters greater psychological safety and deeper trust.

7. **Recover Gracefully When You Miss**

   Even seasoned leaders sometimes misread the room or choose the wrong approach. What matters most in those moments is how you recover. A simple statement like,

   "That didn't come out quite right, let me try again," can rebuild rapport and show that you value the relationship more than your ego.

   Servant leaders don't fear mistakes in communication; they use them to learn and connect more deeply.

A Practice Challenge

To build your own adaptable communication practice, consider this challenge over the next week:

- Identify two or three team members who have different communication styles than your own.
- Observe how they typically respond; do they prefer brief summaries or full context? Do they engage more in writing or verbally?

- Choose one upcoming interaction with each person and consciously adjust your tone, delivery method, or structure.
- Reflect on how the message was received.
- Ask for feedback: "Was that a helpful way to communicate this?" or "Would another approach have worked better?"

The goal is not to change your identity, but to grow your communication fluency and increase your leadership impact in the process.

Personal Commitment

To anchor this practice, write your own communication commitment. Here's a sample you might adapt:

"I commit to communicating with intentionality, empathy, and flexibility. I will meet people where they are not to impress them, but to connect meaningfully, serve more effectively, and lead with greater impact."

Your Turn: Cultivating Your Communication Chameleon

To grow your own adaptability:

- **Start small.** Pick one upcoming conversation and consciously adjust your tone or format.
- **Observe reactions.** Notice what sparks engagement or resistance.
- **Reflect and adjust.** What worked? What felt forced? What felt natural?
- **Seek feedback.** Invite your team to share how you're landing.
- **Keep practicing.** Adaptability is an ongoing journey, not a one-time fix.

Remember, leadership communication isn't about dazzling everyone with eloquence. It's about connecting meaningfully, so your message can inspire trust, action, and growth.

What Communication Chameleons Never Do

- Speak just to check a box.
- Assume that one-size-fits-all works.
- Blame the listener for not understanding.
- Overtalk or overshare out of insecurity.
- Withhold information as power.

Chameleons use communication not to control, but to connect.

Leadership Language in Action

Imagine these real-world examples:

Scenario	Default Leader	Communication Chameleon
Announcing a change	"New policy starts Monday."	"Here's why we're making this change, how it benefits the team, and what support you'll get."
Giving feedback	"You missed the mark again."	"I noticed a gap in this area—can we talk about what got in the way and how I can help support you going forward?"
Motivating a struggling team	"Let's pick up the pace."	"I know it's been a heavy season. Your resilience has been incredible. Let's talk about what's next, together."

Same goal. Radically different impact.

Reflective Exercise: Unlock Your Communication Adaptability

This three-part exercise will help you gain awareness, identify gaps, and plan a more adaptable approach.

Part 1: Know Your Default

1. **When I need to communicate something important, I usually:**
   ☐ Send an e-mail
   ☐ Call a meeting

- ☐ Drop by for a quick chat
- ☐ Text or Slack
- ☐ Wait until someone asks

2. **My tone tends to be:**
   - ☐ Direct
   - ☐ Encouraging
   - ☐ Detailed
   - ☐ Casual
   - ☐ Cautious
3. **People often respond to me by:**
   - ☐ Nodding but not acting
   - ☐ Asking for clarification
   - ☐ Avoiding follow-up questions
   - ☐ Engaging immediately
   - ☐ Giving emotional feedback

What does this tell you about your current style?
Are you delivering in a way that works for *you* but not for *them*?

Part 2: Reflect on Real Moments

Think of a recent communication win:

- What worked?
- What medium did you use?
- What style did you match?

Now think of a communication miss:

- What didn't land?
- What assumptions did you make about the listener?
- How could you have adjusted?

Part 3: Plan to Adapt

Over the next week, identify two to three people on your team who have different communication styles than yours.

For each one, answer these questions:

- What's their likely style or preference?
- How can I adapt to connect with them better?
- What channel or tone will work best?

Commitment Statement:

"I commit to adapting my communication with intentionality, empathy, and flexibility. I will meet people where they are, so I can lead them where they need to go."

Final Thoughts: Adapt to Connect, Not to Impress

The best leaders don't have one voice; they have a hundred. And they know how and when to use each one.

Being a communication chameleon doesn't mean you're inconsistent; it means you're in tune.

With your team.
With the moment.
With the mission.

So shift the tone. Match the rhythm. Reframe the message. Not to be liked, but to be understood.

Because when you're a servant leader, you're not speaking for yourself. You're speaking for them. Like the chameleon, you don't change who you are, you adjust how you connect, so your message lands where it matters most.

PART IV

Leading With Vision and Magic

CHAPTER 13

Catch the Fly

This chapter explores the subtle yet powerful leadership skill of noticing and addressing small, often overlooked signals the "flies" buzzing quietly beneath the surface of daily work life. Through vivid metaphor and practical guidance, it highlights how servant leaders cultivate presence, curiosity, and follow-through to catch these early warning signs before they escalate. The chapter also expands awareness beyond individuals to include systemic cultural patterns and internal leadership blind spots. Ultimately, it shows how attending to these small moments builds trust, prevents larger issues, and strengthens organizational health.

If you've ever watched *The Karate Kid*, you'll remember the scene: Mr. Miyagi, eyes narrowed, hand steady, is attempting to catch a fly with chopsticks. Daniel, confused, watches this absurd task unfold. It's slow, focused, meticulous, and seemingly impossible.

But this wasn't just about bugs. It was about **Discipline**, **Precision**, **Patience, and Presence**.

Leadership is full of flies: small irritations, subtle cues, and tiny problems with the potential to become major ones. The missed glance in a meeting. The e-mail that reads a little colder than usual. The staff member who used to laugh loudly and now avoids eye contact. These flies don't scream for attention—they buzz just quietly enough to be ignored.

Most leaders swat at them when they're too distracting to overlook. But servant leaders catch them early not with frustration, but with curiosity. They know that leadership isn't only about reacting to crises. It's about sensing the signal before the noise.

What the "Fly" Really Represents

Let's unpack the metaphor. The "fly" is:

- The small behavior shift that goes unspoken.
- The delayed response from a usually prompt colleague.
- The good employee who's suddenly disengaged.
- The small inefficiency that quietly drains hours each week.
- The slight sarcasm that hides hurt under humor.

It's not the fire, it's the smoke. And **servant leaders are smoke detectors.**

Ignoring the fly might seem easier in the moment. But leadership is in the noticing. Flies rarely disappear on their own; they become distractions, disconnections, or deep-seated dysfunction if left unaddressed.

Why Leaders Miss the Fly

1. **We're too focused on the obvious.**
   If it's not a deadline, a fire, or a crisis, we move on. We miss nuance because we're stuck in urgency.
2. **We confuse activity with attentiveness.**
   We think because we're working hard, we're leading well. But leadership isn't just effort, it's awareness.
3. **We tolerate tiny problems.**
   Small annoyances often feel like a leadership "tax." Something we just accept. But the fly we tolerate today becomes the habit we regret tomorrow.
4. **We underestimate our influence.**
   Leaders sometimes assume that someone else will address it. But what we ignore, we endorse.

How Servant Leaders Catch the Fly

1. **They See the Invisible**
   Servant leaders develop what some call *organizational peripheral vision.* They're not just scanning the room; they're reading between the lines.

They notice:

- Who changed seats in the meeting.
- Who stopped contributing.
- Whose humor became more biting than playful.
- Which Slack channels have gone quiet.

They know that small cues reveal big truths.

2. **They Ask Brave, Gentle Questions**

   They don't need drama to initiate dialogue. They lean into discomfort early with empathy.

   They ask:

   - "Hey, I noticed a shift lately. How are you doing?"
   - "Something felt different in that meeting did you feel that too?"
   - "You've been quiet lately. Anything you want to share?"

   These aren't interrogations. They're invitations. An open door, not a spotlight.

3. **They Follow Up**

   Catching a fly is one thing. Making sure it doesn't come back is leadership. Servant leaders don't stop at awareness that they follow through.

   They document. They follow up. They change systems. They rebuild trust. They do the unseen work that keeps culture from slowly leaking air.

Real-Life Story: The Fly That Became a Bridge

There was a hospital administrator, we'll call him Marcus, who noticed a nurse who had once been highly engaged now seemed distracted. At first, he rationalized it. "She's probably tired." But something lingered.

Instead of brushing it off, Marcus pulled her aside and asked: "You don't feel like yourself lately, want to talk?"

That conversation revealed something; no one knew that she had just experienced a miscarriage and returned to work before she was ready. Her body was back, but her heart was still grieving. The workplace didn't demand answers, but Marcus's simple question gave her space to be seen.

That day, he didn't just catch the fly he caught her before she fell.

The Cost of an Uncaught Fly

For every disengaged team member, there's usually a moment that was missed.
A leader looked away.
A comment went unaddressed.
An apology wasn't made.
A process glitch became accepted.

Gallup research shows that 85 percent of employees worldwide are not engaged or are actively disengaged at work, and early signs of disengagement (withdrawal, decreased participation, mood changes) are often missed until performance drops.

Culture erosion doesn't happen in explosions; it happens in increments.

Flies in the Culture: Systems and Self

Some flies aren't about individuals they're baked into the culture. Others buzz quietly inside our own leadership habits.

Systemic Flies:

- **Outdated onboarding** that overwhelms new hires.
- **Noninclusive meeting norms** where the same voices dominate.
- **Recognition systems** that reward output but ignore effort.
- **Unspoken norms** that discourage vulnerability from parents, caregivers, or underrepresented team members.

A study published in the *Harvard Business Review* found that unresolved small workplace conflicts, when ignored, can escalate to affect up to 25 percent of an employee's time in lost productivity and stress management. These don't announce themselves with alarms. But servant leaders notice the friction and choose to name it, question it, and change it.

Internal Flies:

- Avoiding feedback conversations to "keep the peace."
- Dismissing your own discomfort instead of exploring it.
- Brushing off leadership habits that don't serve your team.

The hardest fly to catch is the one in your own blind spot. But self-awareness is the foundation of real leadership growth. You can't fix what you won't face.

The Fly as a Mirror

Every fly you notice or fail to notice is a reflection. Not just of your team, but of yourself as a leader. Flies are mirrors of culture, values, and energy. They whisper: *"Here is what matters here, and here is what we tolerate."*

The disengaged glance, the overlooked idea, the quiet frustration; they all reveal what your team feels safe noticing, safe speaking up about, and safe expecting from leadership. The fly doesn't just show a problem; it reveals the gaps between **intentions** and **realities**.

Ask yourself:

- What does it say about my leadership when this fly was ignored?
- What signals do my daily actions send about what's valued and what isn't?
- Am I fostering a culture where small concerns are caught early, or swept under the rug until they grow?

The beauty and the challenge is that the fly isn't a moral judgment. It's data. A signal. A chance to align action with values. Leaders who treat flies as mirrors can:

- Reframe small problems as opportunities to reinforce trust.
- Adjust systems before they become sources of stress or disengagement.
- Model the attention, care, and presence they wish to see in others.

In this way, every fly caught is a leadership statement: *I see. I care. I will act.* Missed flies, in contrast, silently shape norms that become harder to change over time. The fly, then, is not just a warning; it's feedback, reflection, and opportunity all in one.

The Ripple Effect of Catching One Fly

Don't underestimate how much trust you build by addressing one small thing.

- The junior team member you check in on becomes a future leader who remembers how it felt to be seen.
- The seemingly trivial workflow change makes your team 10 percent more energized.
- The one word you rephrase in a difficult conversation changes the entire tone.

Catching the fly may seem insignificant today, but it may be the *reason someone stays tomorrow.*

The Stillness Between the Buzz

Most leaders are trained to respond, not to *notice.* We rush to solve, fix, and move forward. But catching the fly isn't about quick reflexes, it's about inner stillness.

When Mr. Miyagi poised his chopsticks, he wasn't frantically swatting. He was *centered.* His calm created clarity. The same is true in leadership: the more chaotic the environment, the more stillness we need to see what others miss. Servant leadership begins not with doing, but with being present enough to sense the subtle energy shifts in a room, the unspoken tension in a meeting, or the quiet fatigue behind a forced smile.

Stillness sharpens perception. When we slow down, we begin to notice:

- The way laughter sounds different when morale is fading.
- The tone of an e-mail that reveals frustration more than words admit.

- The moment someone's enthusiasm fades after being interrupted.
- The breath a team member takes before agreeing to something they don't want to do.

These aren't management metrics, they're energetic cues. And they require a leader who leads from awareness, not assumption.

To catch the fly, you must first quiet the noise within.

When your mind is racing, you only see what confirms your urgency. But when you ground yourself, take a breath before responding, observe before reacting; the small truths emerge. The fly reveals itself.

Practical ways to cultivate this stillness in daily leadership:

1. **Pause before you enter a room.** Take one deep breath and set the intention to *notice before speaking.*
2. **Listen to the energy, not just the words.** What's not being said often matters most.
3. **End your day with reflection, not reaction.** Ask: "What did I sense today that I didn't act on?"
4. **Protect quiet thinking time.** Your best leadership insights rarely appear in meetings; they surface in moments of stillness.

Leadership isn't only about catching what's visible. It's about tuning your presence until the invisible becomes undeniable.

Because the truth is, the fly never appears to those moving too fast to see it.

Awareness without action is observation, not leadership. The stillness that helps you notice the fly must lead to motion; intentional, humble, human motion. Servant leaders don't pause just to reflect; they pause to respond better. They translate awareness into small, meaningful steps that ripple through relationships, systems, and self. Practice isn't perfection, its presence in motion.

Action Commitment: Catching Flies This Week

This week, choose three ways to practice this:

1. **Fly of Relationship**: Check in with one person whose energy seems off.

2. **Fly of System**: Identify one low-friction problem and bring it to your team for a collaborative solution.
3. **Fly of Self**: Journal about a recent leadership moment where you avoided something small and what you'll do differently next time.

Then declare:

This week, I will catch the fly by noticing what others might ignore, asking what others avoid, and caring when it's easiest not to.

Final Thought: Small Things Become Big Things

Catching a fly with chopsticks might look silly. But maybe that's the point. Leadership isn't always about grand strategy or keynote speeches.

Sometimes, it's about **leaning in when most lean out.**

Noticing when others don't.

Asking when it's awkward.

And showing up not just when things break—but when they're *starting* to bend.

Catch the fly.

Because the best leaders don't just fight fires.

They prevent the sparks.

Sometimes the fly isn't just something *wrong*, it's something *missing*.

It's the idea someone didn't share.

The compliment you meant to give but never said.

The gratitude that remained unspoken.

The encouragement that could've made the difference.

Catching the fly is not only about fixing what's broken; it's about *noticing what's needed.*

That extra 30 seconds of presence.

That "How are you, really?"

That "Thank you, I see what you did."

It's small. But it's everything.

So, pause. Pay attention. Then act.

Because the fly might just be the very thing someone's spirit is waiting on.

Reflection Exercise: Seeing the Fly as a Mirror

This week, take 15 minutes at the end of each day to reflect on the "flies" you noticed—and what they revealed about your team, culture, and leadership. Use this simple three-step framework:

1. **Observe:** Write down one small cue you noticed today; a behavior, comment, or energy shift that felt significant.
   Example: "During the meeting, Lisa avoided eye contact when her project was discussed."
2. **Interpret:** Ask yourself what this fly reflects. Is it a sign of disengagement, a process flaw, or a gap in communication? Avoid judgment; focus on insight.
   Example: "She might feel her input isn't valued, or she's overwhelmed with workload."
3. **Act:** Identify one small action to address it to support your team, improve the system, or model the leadership behavior you want to see.
   Example: "I'll check in privately with Lisa tomorrow and ask how she's managing her workload and what support she might need."

Daily Commitment Statement

"This week, I will use the small signals I notice as mirrors; to understand, reflect, and act in ways that reinforce trust and strengthen culture."

CHAPTER 14

The Process Was Fine, but Ferris Bueller Had the Right Vibe

This chapter explores the powerful role of "vibe" in leadership and organizational culture, showing why energy and emotional connection often matter more than process alone. Through the example of Ferris Bueller's charismatic leadership style, it illustrates how vibe shapes engagement, creativity, and loyalty. You'll learn how to balance structure with human connection, cultivate sustainable positive energy within your team, and apply practical strategies and reflections to elevate your leadership presence. Ultimately, the chapter emphasizes that while processes keep things running, it's the vibe that inspires people to show up fully and thrive.

> "Life moves pretty fast. If you don't stop and look around once in a while, you could miss it." —*Ferris Bueller*

The 1986 film *Ferris Bueller's Day Off* isn't just a classic teen comedy; it's a masterclass in the power of vibe. Ferris Bueller, the charismatic high school senior, doesn't just bend the rules; he radiates an energy that makes everyone around him lean in, lighten up, and step outside the grind. He didn't rewrite the rules. He changed the game by shifting the energy.

In many ways, Ferris is the leader we all wish we had—confident without arrogance, playful without being careless, influential without ever needing a title. And most importantly, he created an experience. His "day off" was unforgettable, not because of its structure or efficiency, but because of its *vibe.*

In business and leadership, we often obsess over process. But process alone doesn't create passion, momentum, or loyalty. Culture does. And culture is vibe made visible.

The Role of Process: Necessary but Not Sufficient

Processes are the backbone of any successful operation. They provide consistency. They reduce waste. They help new employees onboard, deliver quality at scale, and keep the trains running on time.

In high-performing organizations, well-designed processes do the following:

- Prevent ambiguity by offering clarity of expectations.
- Free up cognitive load by creating reliable systems.
- Create equity and fairness in workflows.
- Make excellence replicable and not dependent on individual heroics.

But here's where it breaks down: **when the process becomes the purpose**, rather than the support structure. When people start serving the process instead of using the process to serve people.

It's like building a beautiful airport terminal but forgetting to invite anyone to fly. Processes can carry people to purpose but only when they're animated by vibe.

Why Vibe Outranks Process Every Time

Vibe is hard to define but easy to feel. It's the emotional pulse of a team. It's what people say when leadership isn't in the room. It's how meetings feel. It's the intangible "something" that makes a job feel joyful or soul-crushing.

Here's what a great vibe creates:

- **Engagement**: People want to show up not because they have to, but because they get to.
- **Momentum**: Things move forward without being pushed. People volunteer ideas, energy, and time.
- **Creativity**: The freedom to experiment, laugh, and speak openly produces innovation.
- **Loyalty**: People stay where they're *seen*, not just where they're *paid*.

Research by Gallup (2020) shows that teams with higher employee engagement a proxy for positive energy and vibe, experience 21 percent greater profitability, 17 percent higher productivity, and 41 percent lower absenteeism compared to disengaged teams.

Vibe is a leader's silent megaphone. People follow energy more than direction. They respond more to your presence than your process manual. Great vibes aren't accidental, they're cultivated.

The Science Behind Vibe: How Energy Shapes Teams

Vibe isn't just a "soft skill" or a nice-to-have feeling; it has measurable effects on behavior, decision making, and organizational outcomes. Understanding the mechanics of energy gives leaders a framework to intentionally cultivate it.

Emotional Contagion: Energy Spreads Like a Wave

Humans unconsciously mirror the emotions of those around them. Facial expressions, tone of voice, posture, and overall energy are absorbed by team members, often faster than formal instructions.

Insight: A leader's positive energy can cascade through a team, just as stress or negativity can. Energy is invisible, but its effects are immediate.

Motivation Through Connection

Self-Determination Theory shows that people thrive when they feel autonomous, competent, and connected. Vibe impacts all three:

- **Autonomy:** Encourages experimentation and creative problem-solving.
- **Competence:** Recognizes effort and contribution in real time.
- **Relatedness:** Strengthens bonds through warmth and engagement.

Processes alone rarely satisfy these intrinsic motivators—vibe does.

Flow and Cognitive Load

High-stress or rigid environments drain mental resources. Positive energy reduces friction, allowing teams to focus, innovate, and enter "flow" states where work feels effortless and ideas emerge naturally.

Cultural Signaling

Processes define *what* to do. Energy communicates *how* and *why*. Teams pick up on the tone of leadership faster than rules, shaping everyday behaviors and attitudes in subtle but powerful ways.

Resilience and Adaptability

Vibe isn't just about fun or engagement; it builds a team's capacity to handle challenges. Positive energy fosters psychological safety, encouraging risk-taking, learning from mistakes, and bouncing back faster from setbacks.

Vibe is a lever of human behavior. Leaders who understand it aren't relying on charisma or luck; they're designing an environment where people consistently show up fully, collaborate effectively, and stay engaged over the long term.

Ferris Bueller: A Lesson in Leading With Vibe

Let's break down why Ferris worked:

- **Confidence without control**: He trusted himself and invited others to join, not forced them.
- **Relationships before rules**: Ferris connected before he instructed. He cared about people's experiences.
- **Improve over rigidity**: He wasn't reckless, he was responsive. He stayed fluid in the face of structure.
- **Joy as a leadership value**: The ultimate vibe-giver. Ferris prioritized fun and made it contagious.

In your own leadership, you don't need to throw away structure. You just need to humanize it. The vibe is what brings your systems to life.

Extended Case Study: When the Vibe Brings the Process Back to Life

Let's take the veterinary clinic example further. After installing a near-perfect digital appointment system, the staff became robotic. Clients missed the warmth they used to feel at the front desk. Morale began to dip.

Leadership didn't scrap the system. Instead, they:

- Assigned "client vibe leads" for each shift someone responsible for the *emotional* tone.
- Added "wiggle room" into the schedule slots for extended conversations or recovery time.
- Began weekly "Vibe Check" huddles to discuss moments of connection or disconnection from the week.
- Encouraged storytelling: team members shared how their work made a difference in a pet's life that week.

The result? Same process. Better energy. And that changed everything from client satisfaction to employee retention.

How Servant Leaders Create Vibe That Sticks

Anyone can bring good energy once. Servant leaders create environments where it's sustainable.

A study in the *Journal of Organizational Behavior* found that a leader's emotional tone accounts for up to 70 percent of the variance in a team's emotional climate, which in turn strongly predicts collaboration, creativity, and retention.

Here's how:

1. **Build Emotional Intelligence Into the Process**
   Design team rituals that check in on how people *feel*, not just what they've done. Ask:
   "What's your energy like today?" or
   "What's one thing we can shift to make work better this week?"

2. **Train for Tone, Not Just Tasks**
   New hire onboarding should include not just *what* we do but *how we show up*. Help them understand your culture's tone, humor, kindness, and expectations of empathy.
3. **Design Spaces That Match the Vibe**
   This could be as simple as turning off fluorescent lights, adding music to the office, or creating "no-meeting zones" on calendars. Space affects energy.
4. **Protect the Positivity**
   Negativity is contagious but so is enthusiasm. When team members bring toxic energy, deal with it. You can't have a good vibe with unaddressed dysfunction in the corner.

Sustaining the Vibe: Beyond Short Bursts of Energy

Injecting energy occasionally is easy; sustaining it consistently is the real leadership challenge. Long-term vibe requires intentional design, reflection, and follow-through. Here's how to keep the momentum alive without burning out your team or yourself:

1. **Embed Vibe Into Rituals**
   Create recurring practices that reinforce your culture's energy, such as:
   - Weekly check-ins that highlight wins and challenges.
   - Monthly storytelling sessions to share moments of impact.
   - Quarterly team celebrations that honor both effort and results.
2. **Balance Energy With Recovery**
   High energy is contagious but if it comes at the cost of exhaustion, it won't last. Encourage breaks, time off, and flexibility. Leaders who model balance set the tone for sustainable engagement.
3. **Coach for Emotional Agility**
   Equip your team to navigate stress, setbacks, and change without losing their positive energy. Emotional agility helps maintain vibe even when processes get messy or deadlines loom.

4. **Measure More Than Metrics**
   Track the health of your culture, not just KPIs. Surveys, one-on-one conversations, and informal observations reveal whether the vibe is thriving, stagnant, or slipping.
5. **Celebrate the Invisible Wins**
   Recognize moments where vibe made the difference; like a client leaving happier than expected, or a team solving a problem creatively. These reinforce that energy, not just output, drives success.

A great vibe isn't a one-off event, it's a sustainable, living element of leadership. Leaders who treat it as an asset to nurture will see engagement, creativity, and loyalty compound over time, creating a culture that attracts and retains the best people naturally.

Practical Microvibe Shifts to Sustain Positive Energy

Now that you've explored how to embed vibe into rituals, protect it from burnout, and reinforce it through reflection, here are actionable ways to put it into practice this week. These microshifts are small but compounding; they keep your team's energy alive and aligned with your culture:

- **Theme Days With Purpose:** Funky Sock Friday isn't just fun; it creates a shared, playful ritual. Consider adding a short reflection: "Why did this make us smile this week?" to tie joy back to culture.
- **Surprise Gratitude Shoutouts:** Highlight someone's impact in the moment. Connect it to the bigger picture so recognition becomes part of the culture, not just a one-off.
- **Start Meetings With "High/Low":** Share one high moment and one challenge. Doing this consistently builds emotional agility and keeps everyone aware of the team's pulse.
- **Ask the "Ferris Question":** "If you could do anything today to bring joy to the team, what would it be?" Make it a recurring check-in rather than a one-off prompt; small experiments compound into lasting engagement.

- **Microcelebrations of Invisible Wins:** Notice moments where vibe made a difference; a client interaction, a problem solved creatively, or a team member lifting someone's energy. Recognize them publicly or privately to reinforce the positive loop.

Leadership Commitment Prompt

This week, I will _____________ to elevate the energy and bring more of the Ferris Bueller vibe into our culture. Because leading isn't about control—it's about connection.

Reflective Exercise: Discover and Elevate Your Leadership Vibe

Set aside 30–40 minutes in a quiet space with a journal or digital note app. Reflect on these prompts:

1. **Vibe Audit**
   - How would I describe the current vibe of my team or organization? Use three words.
   - What behaviors, attitudes, or traditions contribute to this vibe?
   - Are there processes or policies that might be dampening the vibe?
2. **Personal Vibe Reflection**
   - When do I feel most "in the zone" as a leader; authentic, energized, connected?
   - What energy do I bring into my daily interactions?
   - How do others respond to my vibe?
3. **Ferris Bueller Moment**
   - Recall a time when you embodied the "Ferris Bueller vibe"; confident, spontaneous, and magnetic. What made that moment work?
   - How can you bring more of that energy into your leadership today?

4. **Action Plan**
   Choose one small, specific action you can take this week to infuse a more positive vibe into your leadership, such as:
   - Starting meetings with a quick gratitude round.
   - Allowing flexibility in a rigid process to better serve your team.
   - Sharing a personal story or vulnerability in a team check-in.

Write your commitment:

"This week, I will _________ to bring more of the 'right vibe' into my leadership because process alone isn't enough."

Final Thought: Culture Eats Process for Breakfast

You can have the most flawless process on paper, but without the right vibe, it will never unlock the full potential of your team or business.

Ferris Bueller's day off reminds us: people respond to *energy*, *authenticity*, and *connection*. When you lead with the right vibe, you don't just manage systems you inspire lives.

So, as you navigate the balance between process and people, remember: the process was fine, but Ferris had the right vibe and that's what made all the difference.

Because when the process is good, but vibe is great, people don't just follow you; they **feel something from you**. And that feeling? That's what keeps them coming back, keeps them caring, and keeps them giving their best.

CHAPTER 15

Just like Walt, It's All About Faith, Trust, and Pixie Dust

This chapter explores how the timeless leadership principles embodied by Walt Disney—faith, trust, and a touch of "pixie dust"—can transform organizational culture. It highlights the power of believing in people and purpose before results show, building trust through empowerment and consistency, and infusing everyday work with joy and meaningful connection. Through these elements, leaders can create vibrant, resilient cultures that inspire engagement, creativity, and lasting loyalty. Ultimately, the chapter shows how leading with vision and heart turns ordinary workplaces into places where magic happens and legacies are built.

> "All our dreams can come true, if we have the courage to pursue them."
>
> —Walt Disney

In the world of business, it's easy to get caught up in metrics, profits, and the never-ending hustle of quarterly results. Leaders are pushed to prioritize bottom lines over belief systems, structure over soul. But if we pull back the curtain, we often find that what truly sustains great companies isn't just a robust business model, it's culture. And not just any culture, but one rooted in vision, belief, and a little bit of magic. Or as Walt Disney would put it: **faith, trust, and pixie dust**.

This chapter explores how embracing Walt's philosophy can serve as a powerful foundation for building a servant leadership-driven, positive business culture. These aren't just idealistic notions; they are strategic elements for long-term impact. Let's break them down and explore how they show up, not only in theme parks but also in the halls, offices, Zoom calls, and Slack channels of the organizations we lead.

Faith: Believing Before You See

Walt Disney's empire began with little more than a mouse, a sketchpad, and relentless belief. He saw a world that didn't yet exist and refused to be deterred by rejection, resistance, or rational limitations. That kind of visionary faith is at the heart of servant leadership.

For leaders today, faith means:

- **Faith in People**: We choose to believe in the capability, creativity, and character of our team members not because they've already proven themselves, but because we see their potential. Sometimes, the greatest gift you can give someone is to believe in them before they believe in themselves. A global study by LinkedIn (2022) found that 79 percent of employees say they would stay longer at a company that invests in their growth and potential, even before the results are fully visible.
- **Faith in the Mission**: Culture suffers when vision is absent. Servant leaders are keepers of the mission, reminding their teams why the work matters. When belief drives behavior, excellence follows.
- **Faith in the Process**: Progress is often invisible at first. Cultural transformation, team development, and long-term results take time. Faith means resisting the temptation to rush, micromanage, or overcorrect. It's choosing steady intention over frantic reaction.

Walt once said, "It's kind of fun to do the impossible." That fun doesn't come from playing it safe; it comes from having the courage to lead with belief, even in uncertainty.

Trust: The Currency of Culture

If faith is the spark, trust is the structure. Walt trusted the people around him—animators, architects, and engineers—to take big ideas and make them real. He understood that innovation requires freedom, and freedom requires trust.

In the modern workplace, trust shows up in tangible and subtle ways:

- **Psychological Safety**: People won't speak freely if they're afraid of being shut down or penalized. Servant leaders create environments where mistakes are seen as learning moments, not failures.
- **Empowerment**: Leaders who trust their teams let go of control and offer autonomy. They give team members the room to make decisions, try new things, and take risks knowing that even if it doesn't work, growth will still occur.
- **Integrity and Consistency**: Nothing destroys trust faster than inconsistency. If you say you care about well-being, but overwork your team every week, you create dissonance. Servant leaders align their actions with their values. They show up consistently and humbly.

Gallup (2023) reports that employees who strongly trust their leaders are four times more likely to be engaged and that high-trust cultures see 50 percent higher productivity and significantly lower turnover. Trust takes time to build and seconds to break. It's not something you demand; it's something you demonstrate, one small, intentional act at a time.

Pixie Dust: The Magic of Culture

Faith and trust create the foundation, but pixie dust is what brings it to life. It's the intangible energy that makes a workplace feel different. It's what your people feel, not just what they do. It's the moments that make work feel meaningful, not mechanical.

Pixie dust might sound whimsical, but it's deeply strategic. Here's what it can look like:

- **Moments of Delight**: Think birthday shoutouts, themed team meetings, surprise coffee gift cards, or handwritten

thank-you notes. These aren't distractions from the work; they're reminders of humanity within it.
- **Emotional Connection**: Real culture can't exist without real relationships. Pixie dust shows up when you know your teammates' kids' names, ask about their passions, or remember the little things that matter.
- **Rituals and Traditions**: Maybe it's Friday shoutouts, Monday check-ins, or monthly celebrations. Intentional rituals bond people together and bring rhythm to the culture.
- **Shared Joy**: Whether it's laughter during a meeting, inside jokes, or storytelling around shared wins, joy is an accelerant for engagement. Servant leaders don't shy away from joy; they protect and promote it.

Pixie dust doesn't replace strategy, systems, or structure; it enhances them. It keeps the spark alive. Without it, even the best-run organizations can feel cold and transactional.

The Ripple Effect: How Belief Shapes Behavior

Faith, trust, and pixie dust aren't just abstract ideals, they are behavioral catalysts that ripple through an organization in profound ways. When leaders embody these principles, their influence spreads far beyond direct reports, shaping interactions, norms, and decision making throughout the culture.

Belief Begets Engagement

When leaders demonstrate faith in people's potential, it signals that growth is possible and mistakes are part of the journey. This doesn't just inspire confidence; it changes behavior. Employees are more likely to take initiative, suggest creative solutions, and persist in the face of challenges.

Trust Multiplies Leadership

Trust isn't merely a feeling; it's a force multiplier. In high-trust cultures, decision making accelerates because people rely on one another rather than waiting for approval at every turn. Errors become learning moments, collaboration flourishes, and accountability strengthens. Leaders who consciously build trust effectively decentralize leadership, creating an environment where initiative and ownership thrive at every level.

Pixie Dust as Cultural Glue

The whimsical "magic" of culture, rituals, shared joy, and meaningful surprises—serves a functional purpose: it binds people emotionally to the organization and to each other. Neuroscience research shows that positive experiences release dopamine and oxytocin, which increase trust, creativity, and memory retention. Pixie dust isn't fluff; it is the emotional glue that makes vision and values stick. A simple act of recognition or a shared laugh can reinforce the belief and trust already seeded, creating a feedback loop where culture becomes self-sustaining.

The Multiplier Effect

When faith, trust, and pixie dust are intentionally practiced, they amplify one another. Belief encourages risk-taking, which builds trust when people follow through. Trust fosters deeper connection, which makes moments of magic resonate more strongly. The result is a culture where engagement, innovation, and loyalty aren't occasional, they are the default.

The magic isn't just in grand gestures or inspirational quotes; it's in the small, deliberate actions that leaders take every day. Each moment of belief, each demonstration of trust, each spark of joy ripples outward, influencing not just performance, but the way people feel about their work, their teams, and the organization itself. In this way, culture becomes both a product and a process, something created intentionally and experienced tangibly, a living legacy that grows long after any individual leader has moved on.

Sprinkle the Ripple: Practical Ways to Amplify Faith, Trust, and Pixie Dust

- **Spot and Celebrate Potential:** Recognize not just results, but effort, creativity, and growth. Give encouragement before outcomes are visible.

- **Delegate With Confidence:** Give team members meaningful autonomy. Step back and let them lead where appropriate, trust in their judgment.
- **Make Small Moments Count:** Handwritten notes, shoutouts, or spontaneous coffee runs aren't fluff, they reinforce connection and joy.
- **Share Stories of Success and Setbacks:** Normalize learning and show how faith and trust lead to real growth.
- **Create Mini-Rituals:** Start meetings with gratitude rounds, end weeks with highlights, or establish fun traditions. Consistency + joy = culture glue.
- **Lead with Curiosity:** Ask questions, listen deeply, and stay open to ideas; your engagement signals belief in others' contributions.

Leading Like Walt

Walt Disney wasn't flawless, but he led with an unapologetic blend of creativity, courage, and care. He dared to imagine a different kind of world and then brought others along for the ride.

To lead like Walt, embrace these servant-leader practices:

1. **Cast Vision Boldly**: Don't manage with caution, lead with courage. Share your dream and let people rally around it.
2. **Connect Every Role to Purpose**: Remind every person how their work matters. Whether they're sweeping the floors or shaping the strategy, their contribution counts.
3. **Coach, Don't Command**: Help people grow. Equip, encourage, and empower them even if that means they someday leave your team for a bigger opportunity.
4. **Design Culture Deliberately**: Don't wait for your culture to form. Shape it with rituals, symbols, language, and values that reflect what matters most.

From Fantasyland to the Frontlines

Every organization has the potential to be someone's "Magic Kingdom," a place where they feel seen, stretched, and supported. But that magic doesn't build itself. You must show up for it. Daily. Intentionally.

Culture isn't crafted in slogans or spreadsheets. It's created in moments the way you respond to failure, the way you celebrate wins, the way you show up in a crisis. Magic happens not just in keynote speeches or retreats; it happens in e-mails, 1:1s, team huddles, and hallway conversations.

So, lead with belief. Build with trust. And sprinkle in the kind of joyful, unexpected magic that reminds people: this isn't just work, it's something worth believing in.

Because when you lead with **faith, trust, and pixie dust**, you're not just creating culture.

You're creating legacy.

Exercise: Building Your Culture of Magic

Objective: Translate the principles of faith, trust, and pixie dust into actionable behaviors that ripple through your team or organization.

Time Required: 30–45 minutes

Materials Needed: Pen and paper or a digital note-taking tool

Step 1: Map Your Current Culture (5–10 minutes)

- List three recent moments where your team felt inspired, trusted, or joyful.
- List three recent moments where your team may have felt unsupported, micromanaged, or disengaged.
- Reflect: What patterns do you notice? Where is faith, trust, or pixie dust already present? Where is it missing?

Step 2: Identify Your "Ripple Actions" (10–15 minutes)

- For **Faith**: Pick one person or team whose potential you want to invest in. Write down one concrete action you can take this week to show belief before results.

- For **Trust**: Identify one task or decision you can delegate fully this week. Note how you will communicate confidence and support.
- For **Pixie Dust**: Plan one small, unexpected gesture of joy or connection for your team. It could be a shoutout, a fun ritual, or a personal note.

Step 3: Commit to Action (5 minutes)

- Write down one sentence for each principle that captures your commitment. Example:
  - Faith: "I will celebrate Sarah's initiative on the project, even if the results aren't perfect."
  - Trust: "I will let Raj lead the client presentation without reviewing every slide."
  - Pixie Dust: "I will start Friday's meeting with a two-minute story highlighting a team win."

Step 4: Reflect and Adjust (10–15 minutes, weekly)

- At the end of each week, ask yourself:
  - What worked? What didn't?
  - How did my actions ripple through the team?
  - What can I tweak next week to deepen belief, trust, or joy?

Outcome: By intentionally practicing small, high-leverage behaviors, you will start to see faith, trust, and pixie dust ripple through your team, creating a more vibrant, resilient, and magical culture.

CHAPTER 16

3D Glasses

This chapter introduces the concept of 3D leadership, a transformative approach that expands leadership beyond tasks and management to include deeper self-awareness, genuine relationships, and a clear connection to mission. By viewing leadership through three dimensions of self, people, and mission; leaders can cultivate empathy, clarity, and purpose in their daily actions. Practical tools, reflective questions, and real-world examples guide readers to lead with depth, authenticity, and impact, inspiring teams to grow, trust, and thrive.

Remember the first time you put on 3D glasses at a movie theater?

What looked like a flat screen just moments before suddenly had depth. Characters leapt off the screen. The world expanded. You didn't just watch the story; you were *inside* it.

That's what transformational leadership feels like. When you lead in 3D, you move beyond reacting to tasks or managing people you begin to *see* in layers. You see nuance. You notice signals beneath the surface. You become immersed in the full experience of leading others with empathy, clarity, and conviction.

3D leadership is more than a metaphor. It's a mindset. It means recognizing that leadership isn't just what you *do,* it's how you *see.*

The best leaders don't operate in black and white. They navigate in full color. They read the room, the individual, and the organizational context all at once. They adjust, respond, and reflect in real time.

The Three Dimensions of Servant Leadership

Think of 3D leadership as having three lenses:

1. **The Personal Perspective (the Self)**
2. **The Relational Perspective (the People)**
3. **The Organizational Perspective (the Mission)**

When you lead in 3D, you don't just glance at problems you look *through* them. You don't just manage behavior, you understand *why* it's happening. You don't just focus on outputs you prioritize outcomes that align with *purpose*.

Let's put on those glasses.

The First Dimension: Leading Yourself

This is the lens most leaders skip. They're so focused on fixing things *out there* that they forget the biggest leadership variable is always *within*.

Self-awareness is the difference between reactive leadership and responsive leadership. Research from Korn Ferry found that leaders with high self-awareness are significantly more effective and contribute to stronger organizational performance; in fact, companies with higher rates of self-aware leaders consistently outperform those with lower rates in financial metrics. It's the key to clarity, consistency, and emotional integrity. Without it, your leadership becomes a projection of your stress, ego, and fears, not a reflection of your values.

Ask yourself:

- What's driving my decisions today: fear, habit, ego, or purpose?
- Am I clear on my values, or am I just reacting to pressure?
- Where am I depleted, and am I willing to admit it?
- Am I modeling calm and courage or chaos and control?

Remember: You are always setting the tone. You're the emotional thermostat for your team. If you're scattered, they'll feel it. If you're grounded, they'll rise to meet you.

Servant leadership starts here not in your skillset, but in your *self-set*.

The Second Dimension: Leading People

Once you've checked your own lens, it's time to focus on others. But not just as workers. As people.

This dimension is about *presence* not performance. It's where empathy and leadership intersect.

Too many leaders treat people like functions: the project manager, the analyst, the new hire. 3D leaders see the human behind the role. They lead with curiosity, not assumption.

Here's what 3D relational leadership sounds like:

- "What's something I wouldn't know about you from your resume?"
- "What's been weighing on you lately?"
- "How can I support you beyond work deadlines?"
- "What's one way I can lead you more personally?"

When you lead this way, you stop managing behavior and start nurturing potential. Trust deepens. Psychological safety increases. People show up differently because they know *you* do.

People don't grow from pressure. They grow from *being seen.*

The Third Dimension: Leading the Mission

This is where clarity becomes contagious.

When the vision isn't clear, teams drift into busyness and burnout. Meetings become tasks. Tasks become checkboxes. Energy disappears. Culture flatlines.

3D leaders keep purpose front and center not just at all-hands meetings or annual retreats, but *every day.*

They connect the dots:

- "Here's how your role impacts our client's experience."
- "That feedback you gave helped us grow."
- "This work matters because we're building something bigger than ourselves."

3D leadership reminds people *why* they're here. It fuels meaning in the mundane. A McKinsey study (2021) reported that employees who say they live their purpose at work are 6.5 times more likely to report higher resilience, 4 times more likely to be engaged, and 6 times more likely to stay at their company than those who don't.

When your team is aligned to purpose, work becomes more than effort. It becomes *energy*.

3D Leadership in Motion: A Real-Life Lens

Let's revisit our earlier scenario: A team member is consistently late for meetings.

- **1D Leader (Self Only):**
  "This makes me look bad. I'll issue a warning."
- **2D Leader (Self + Relationship):**
  "I'm frustrated, but I care enough to ask what's going on. Is something happening outside of work?"
- **3D Leader (Self + Relationship + Mission):**
  "I'm noticing a pattern. Let's talk. I want to understand what's going on, how I can support you, and how we can stay aligned with our team's values of reliability and respect."

See the shift? 3D leaders use *every moment* as an opportunity to connect not just correct. They ask better questions. They lead from alignment, not authority.

Practicing 3D Leadership Daily

Here are a few practical ways to integrate 3D thinking into your daily rhythm:

1. **Use the 3D Pause**
   Before responding, ask:
   - "What's happening in me right now?" (1D)
   - "What's happening for them?" (2D)
   - "What matters most in this moment?" (3D)
2. **Replace Tasks With Touchpoints**
   When assigning work, don't just say *what* reinforce *why*.
   - "This connects to our mission by …"
   - "Let's reflect on the impact after."

3. **Build Check-In Cadence**

   Try this format regularly:

   - "Here's what I'm feeling or noticing." (1D)
   - "What are you experiencing?" (2D)
   - "Let's connect it back to where we're going." (3D)

Reflective Exercise: Put on Your 3D Glasses

Block 30–40 minutes this week to reflect on the following lenses. Use them privately or with a trusted coach, peer, or mentor.

Part 1: The 1D Lens—Self

- Where am I leading from fatigue or fear?
- What stories am I telling myself that may not be true?
- What do I need to stay centered this week?

Commitment:

"This week, I will practice stillness by ..."

Part 2: The 2D Lens—People

- Who might be feeling unseen?
- Who do I avoid giving feedback to and why?
- When did I last say, "I believe in you?"

Commitment:

"This week, I'll reach out to ___ with intentional encouragement."

Part 3: The 3D Lens—Mission

- Do we talk about the "why" as much as the "what?"
- Are we aligned or just busy?
- How can I lead with meaning today?

Commitment:

"This month, I'll share one story that reconnects our team to purpose."

Final Scene: Don't Just Look—See

You can lead in gray scale. Many do.

You can lead in logic only. That's common.

But when you choose to lead in 3D, when you bring depth, humanity, and vision into every interaction, you lead in a way that *transforms.*

Your people will notice.
They'll trust you more.
They'll grow with you.
They'll stay longer.
And most importantly, they'll believe in *themselves* because you *saw* them.

That's what happens when you stop looking through a leadership script and start seeing through a servant's heart.

That's what happens when …
you put on your 3D glasses.

Because you were inverted and now, you see the world more clearly than ever before.

The Journey Ahead—Leading Inverted With Purpose and Positivity

As we reach the final pages of this book, take a breath.

You've just spent time rethinking leadership, maybe even unlearning pieces of what you've always been told it's supposed to look like. If you're feeling inspired and challenged, maybe a little uncertain about what comes next good. That means you're doing it right. Because leadership, real leadership, is not a formula. It's not a checklist. It's a living, breathing commitment one that evolves as you do.

Leadership is not a destination; it's a direction. A daily posture. A series of intentional choices are sometimes big, but more often small that build trust, foster belonging, and invite others to grow. And that journey is rarely straight. It's messy. It looks back on itself. It's full of uncertainty, and sometimes self-doubt. But it is always worth it.

This book was never meant to hand you all the answers. It was meant to help you ask better questions. To challenge the myths of leadership you may have inherited. And to offer you a different lens, an inverted one that flips the hierarchy and places people at the center of the mission.

Because the truth is, you don't have to lead from a pedestal. In fact, you're often more effective when you don't.

To be "inverted" in your leadership is not to be weak, soft, or uncertain. It is to be clear-eyed, grounded, and purpose driven. It is to understand that your role as a leader isn't to control outcomes, it's to cultivate conditions. You create a space where growth can happen. Where people feel seen, supported, and empowered to do meaningful work.

And that doesn't come from being the loudest in the room. It comes from listening deeper than anyone else. It doesn't come from pushing people harder. It comes from understanding what truly fuels them and helping them access that fuel. That's what servant leadership is all about.

And it's not idealistic. It's practical. It works. Repeatedly, I've seen it create not just better results, but better humans.

As you've read through these chapters from Bob Ross to Ferris Bueller, Gollum to Ludacris, Walt Disney to The Breakfast Club, you've probably noticed a theme: leadership isn't just about frameworks. It's about feel. Vibe. Energy. Trust. And humor. It's about knowing your people, not just managing them. It's about building culture through the everyday moments, the hallway check-ins, the follow-up messages, the tough but honest feedback, the unexpected encouragement when someone needs it most.

That's where your leadership leaves a legacy.

And here's the beautiful part: You don't have to wait until you "have it all together" to lead this way. You start right where you are imperfect, evolving, learning. You lead anyway. You serve anyway. You show up, even when you don't have all the answers. Especially then.

Because your people don't need you to be perfect. They need you to be present.

The Power of Human-Centered Leadership

In a world that often rewards hustle over health, competition over collaboration, and output over well-being, choosing to lead with empathy and intention can feel radical. But it's not radical, it's responsible. It's necessary. Because the future of leadership isn't about power, it's about people.

And that future starts with you.

You don't need a bigger office or a new title to make an impact. Your impact is made in moments in how you show up, how you respond, and how you invite others to bring their full selves into the room. It's made when you remember that your leadership is never just about business. It's about the lives within the business. The ripple effect you create through the way you make people feel.

Will you be the leader who listens when it's inconvenient?

Who celebrates when there's no spotlight?

Who leads with humility when ego would be easier?

That's the kind of leader the world needs now more than ever.

You have the tools. The insights. The perspective. But more than that, you have the heart.

Don't let perfectionism hold you back. Don't let comparison distract you. And don't let outdated leadership models convince you that you must choose between performance and people. You don't. When you lead with service, when you build with positivity, you ignite both.

So yes, expect the journey to be bumpy. You'll have days where doubt creeps in. Where the weight of leadership feels heavy. Where progress feels slow or invisible. But remember this: You're not alone. And you don't have to do it alone.

Great leaders, inverted leaders don't isolate themselves. They connect. They build trust. They ask for help. They keep the mission centered on us, not me.

The Final Transmission

And that brings me to this: a final, familiar message.

Because sometimes, when the pressure's on, when you're spinning through the chaos of leading teams, building culture, and navigating change, the most important thing you can do is what Maverick did when he wasn't sure he could keep flying:

He reached for his voice of clarity. He said, "Talk to me, Goose."

That line wasn't just about needing information. It was about connections. About grounding. About remembering you're not alone in the cockpit.

So, when you're leading through pressure …
When the mission is unclear …
When you're questioning yourself …
When you feel the weight of responsibility and wonder if you're enough …

Talk to your "Goose."

Find your trusted voice, your mentor, your teammate, your inner compass. Call on those who remind you of who you are and why you lead.

Because leadership is never a solo flight. The best leaders, the bravest leaders, know how to ask for help, to stay connected, and to keep flying even when the skies aren't clear.

And maybe, just maybe … you'll be someone's Goose, too.

So, here's to you, to the leader you are, the one you're becoming, and the people you'll inspire along the way.

Lead with heart.
Lead with courage.
Lead with presence.
Lead inverted.

And when the pressure hits just breathe, steady your hands on the controls, and whisper to yourself … "Talk to me, Goose."

Because that's when you know …
You were born for this.

Bibliography

Association for Applied and Therapeutic Humor. 2021. *Humor in the Workplace: Impact on Creativity and Problem Solving*. AATH Research Brief. https://www.aath.org.

Barsade, Sigal G., and Donald E. Gibson. 2007. "Why Does Affect Matter in Organizations?" *Academy of Management Perspectives* 21, no. 1, pp. 36–59. https://doi.org/10.5465/amp.2007.24286163.

BetterUp. 2019. *Belonging at Work: The Key to Retaining Diverse Talent*. BetterUp Labs. https://www.betterup.com/en-us/resources/reports/belonging-at-work.

Brownell, Judi. 2012. *Listening: Attitudes, Principles, and Skills*. 5th ed. Pearson Higher Ed.

Businessolver. 2021. *State of Workplace Empathy Study*. Businessolver. https://www.businessolver.com/resources/ebooks/state-of-workplace-empathy.

CEB/Gartner. 2016. *Why New Managers Fail*. Arlington, VA: CEB.

Deloitte. 2025. *Deloitte Global 2025 Gen Z and Millennial Survey*. Deloitte Insights. https://www.deloitte.com/global/en/about/press-room/deloitte-2025-gen-z-and-millennial-survey.html.

Deloitte. 2021. *The Equity Imperative: How Inclusion Drives Performance*. Deloitte Insights. https://www2.deloitte.com/

Deloitte. 2022. *Women @ Work: A Global Outlook*. Deloitte Insights. https://www2.deloitte.com/.

Dillon, Blake, and Juliet Bourke. December 16, 2020. "The Value of Belonging at Work." *Harvard Business Review*. https://hbr.org/2020/12/the-value-of-belonging-at-work.

Economist Intelligence Unit. 2018. *Communication Barriers in the Modern Workplace*. The Economist Group. https://eiuperspectives.economist.com/.

Edmondson, Amy. 2019. *The Fearless Organization: Creating Psychological Safety in the Workplace for Learning, Innovation, and Growth*. Wiley.

Gallo, Amy. June 2015. "The Top Complaints from Employees about Their Leaders." *Harvard Business Review*. https://hbr.org/2015/06/the-top-complaints-from-employees-about-their-leaders.

Garton, Eric, and Michael Mankins. March 30, 2017. "The Business Cost of Burnout." *Harvard Business Review*. https://hbr.org/2017/03/the-business-cost-of-burnout.

Gallup. 2021. *Creating Psychological Safety in the Workplace*. Gallup Workplace.

Gallup. 2020. *Employee Engagement and Performance: Latest Insights from Gallup's Meta-Analysis*. Gallup. https://www.gallup.com/workplace/285674/employee-engagement-meta-analysis.aspx.

Gallup. 2017. *State of the American Workplace*. Gallup Press. https://www.gallup.com/workplace/238085/state-american-workplace-report-2017.aspx.

Gallup. 2019. *State of the American Workplace*. Gallup Press.

Gallup. 2022. *State of the Global Workplace: 2022 Report*. Gallup. https://www.gallup.com/workplace/349484/state-of-the-global-workplace-2022-report.aspx.

Gallup. 2023. *State of the Global Workplace: 2023 Report*. Gallup. https://www.gallup.com/workplace/349484/state-of-the-global-workplace.aspx.

Gallup. 2025. *State of the Global Workplace: 2025 Report*. Gallup Workplace. https://www.gallup.com/workplace/.

Gallup. 2017. *State of the Global Workplace*. Gallup Press. https://www.gallup.com/workplace/238079/state-global-workplace-2017.aspx.

Gallup. April 21, 2015. "Why Great Managers Are So Rare." Gallup Workplace .https://news.gallup.com/businessjournal/182792/managers-account-variance-employee-engagement.aspx.

Harvard Business Review. 2016. *The Impact of Toxic Leadership on Trust and Performance*. Harvard Business Publishing.

Harvard Business Review. 2016. *Why Delegating Is So Hard (and What to Do About It)*. Harvard Business Publishing. https://hbr.org.

Harvard Business Review Analytic Services. 2019. *The Business Case for Vulnerability in Leadership*. Boston, MA: Harvard Business Publishing.

Kapur, Manoj. April 24, 2025. "Managers Are Now Disengaged — and That's Costing Companies Big." *Business Insider*. https://www.businessinsider.com/manager-engagement-gallup-workplace-report-2025-4.

Keller, Scott, and Mary Meaney. 2017. *Attracting and Retaining the Right Talent*. McKinsey & Company. https://www.mckinsey.com.

Korn Ferry. 2013. *What Makes a Leader: Why Emotional Intelligence Matters*. Korn Ferry Institute. https://www.kornferry.com/insights/this-week-in-leadership/self-awareness.

Liden, Robert C., Sandy J. Wayne, Chao Liao, and Jeremy D. Meuser. 2020. "Servant Leadership and Team Performance: The Role of Trust and Collaboration." *Leadership & Organization Development Journal* 41, no. 4, pp. 517–529.

LinkedIn. 2022. *2022 Workplace Learning Report: The Transformation of L&D*. LinkedIn Learning. https://learning.linkedin.com/resources/workplace-learning-report.

Lloyd, Kim, Dirk Boer, Jonas Keller, and Sven C. Voelpel. 2015. "Is My Boss Really Listening to Me? The Impact of Perceived Supervisor Listening on Emotional Exhaustion, Turnover Intention, and Organizational Citizenship Behavior." *International Journal of Listening* 29, no. 1, pp. 1–19. https://doi.org/10.1080/10904018.2015.1005564.

Mayo Clinic Staff. 2022. "Stress Relief from Laughter? It's No Joke." *Mayo Clinic.*

McKinsey & Company. 2021. *Help Your Employees Find Purpose—or Watch Them Leave.* McKinsey & Company. https://www.mckinsey.com/business-functions/people-and-organizational-performance/our-insights/help-your-employees-find-purpose-or-watch-them-leave.

Nelson, David L., U.S. Reed, and J.R. Walling. 1976. "Pictorial Superiority Effect." *Journal of Experimental Psychology: Human Learning and Memory* 2, no. 5, pp. 523–528.

Paivio, Allan. 1991. "Dual Coding Theory: Retrospect and Current Status." *Canadian Journal of Psychology* 45, no. 3, pp. 255–287.

The Economic Times. May 6, 2025. "Why Gen Z Is Quietly Rejecting Leadership Roles: Experts Suggest How Companies Can Win Them Back." *The Economic Times.* https://economictimes.indiatimes.com/magazines/panache/why-gen-z-is-quietly-rejecting-leadership-roles-experts-suggest-how-companies-can-win-them-back/articleshow/122455399.cms.

Tubre, Travis C., and James M. Collins. 2000. "Jackson and Schuler (1985) Revisited: A Meta-Analysis of the Relationships Between Role Ambiguity, Role Conflict, and Job Performance." *Journal of Management* 26, no. 1, pp. 155–169.

About the Author

Joshua Schmitz is a leadership strategist, speaker, and culture builder with over 20 years of experience leading teams in the retail, educational, and veterinary industries. As a former vice president of operations and regional operations leader, he has guided hundreds of leaders in transforming their leadership approach and building stronger workplace cultures. Known for blending humor, storytelling, and practical insight, Joshua makes leadership feel approachable and human. His passion lies in helping leaders at every level to create environments where people and performance thrive.

Index

www.ingramcontent.com/pod-product-compliance
Lightning Source LLC
LaVergne TN
LVHW050635100826
845148LV00011B/1873

* 9 7 8 1 6 3 7 4 2 9 6 0 0 *